To Juddi

with very

from

the Author.

NOISES OFF

NOISES OFF

A HANDBOOK OF SOUND EFFECTS

by

FRANK NAPIER

Stage Director at the Old Vic

1931 — 1934

With a Foreword by

TYRONE GUTHRIE

LONDON

FREDERICK MULLER LTD.

29 Great James Street, W.C.1

FIRST PUBLISHED BY FREDERICK MULLER LTD.

IN 1936

PRINTED IN GREAT BRITAIN

BY BUTLER & TANNER LTD.

FROME & LONDON

FOREWORD

I DO not know anyone who knows more about the theory and practice of "Noises Off" than Frank Napier. We worked together for a season at the Old Vic, and during the course of that time we explored many of the possibilities of the Noise-making Art. What I liked about his work was the fact that he was always ripe for experiment. A horsehoof by the river's brim to most Stage-managers is a simple coco-nut and nothing more. Not so to Frank Napier; he will offer you hoofbeat realistic, or, equally readily, hoofbeat surrealistic—the Inner Meaning of the hoofbeat.

Some day I hope to produce a one-act play by Maeterlinck, called "Les Aveugles". The scene is in a dark forest at night. One of the stage directions reads: "The nightbirds exult in the tree-tops." I shall feel that life has not been entirely empty when Frank Napier, requested to produce this effect, does so, immediately and with complete success, aided by an empty matchbox and three bent pins.

TYRONE GUTHRIE.

CONTENTS

vii

CONTENTS

CHAPTER III

CHAPTER IV

CHAPTER V

CONTENTS

CHAPTER VI

CHAPTER VII

CHAPTER VIII

ix

CONTENTS

CHAPTER I

Introductory

IN spite of the very considerable number of books on the theatre and theatrical matters, nothing seems to have been written yet about off-stage sound effects. At any rate, no comprehensive book has been produced which is devoted to this branch of theatrical technique alone. This omission leaves a gap, which should be filled, for the subject is one that needs attention. It may safely be said, that noises off occur in most plays, which is by no means true of period costume. And yet the bibliography of the latter subject is extensive, not to say voluminous.

The discrepancy is doubtless due to the fact that, whereas the design and execution of period costume is guided by rules, which are to be ascertained from the study of historical data, there are no rules, but only a few principles, involved in making noises off, for the problems differ with every play and every theatre. Moreover, period costume can be recorded by description and pictures, but there is no way of writing or drawing an unmusical sound. The data must be collected by the ear and stored in the brain.

The subject of noises off is in itself a fascinating one. It leads the eager practitioner into such varied fields: from the home to the workshop; thence to

I

the aerodrome, and back to the farmyard by way of the battlefield; from the present backward or forward in time; from the commonplace to the fantastical; from the sublime to the ridiculous.

Almost any sound may be required in a play. "There's John now. I heard his key." Simple. Or, in "The Cherry Orchard,"—"A sound is heard that seems to come from the sky, like a breaking harpstring, dying away mournfully." Not quite so simple.

To be a "Public Noise-maker No. 1", therefore, very diverse qualities are needed, and there is practically no end to the studies that will extend the knowledge and improve the technique necessary for this master craft. It shall not be called an art, for that might lead us into attempts to define that provocative word. Thought, however, is free.

In view of the growth of the Amateur Theatre in this country, and since there is no other book on the subject, I hope that this fruit of my somewhat peculiar labours will be of service to many.

As the title implies, this book deals only with sound effects produced off-stage. Music will be excluded, except for passing references, because it does not, or at any rate should not, fall under the category of "noises off". Nor will vocal sounds made by characters, while invisible to the audience, such as sneezes, hysterics, death-cries, and other emotional exclamations, be discussed. These should be classed as "acting", the business of the performers in whose parts they occur, notwithstanding the fact that, upon one occasion, I was called upon to register sudden death for three different characters at a matinée performance, while at another performance that evening I had to produce simultaneously the growls of a bear devouring a gentleman, the cries of the gentleman being devoured, and the yells of an eye-witness, whose upper registers had temporarily deserted him.

Now, there is one obvious aspect of this business of making noises. When the script of a play specifies that certain sounds, germane to the plot, are heard, those sounds must be heard. They have, of course, varying degrees of importance, and should be treated accordingly, just as lines of dialogue are treated, for they are as much parts of the play as are the lines. A knock at the door, or the ringing of a bell, which interrupts a scene, or to which the characters refer, must come as smartly on their cues as the spoken word, or the progress of the play will be held up. The point is obvious and needs no stressing.

But there is another type of sound, which, though asked for or implied in the text, is of such minor importance, such undramatic value, that it may be omitted, if it cannot be successfully produced. Better no sound than a bad sound. For instance, a character may say, "John'll be here in a moment. I heard the car." Now, it is quite conceivable that that character has heard a car, which the audience have not heard, particularly if there has been loud conversation on the stage just before the remark, and if the character acts as though he has heard a slight sound. In such a case, there being no other car effect in the play, it is better to make no sound, when it is considered that the production of a good car effect costs money and/or time and ingenuity. Suppose, on the other hand, that the stage-management makes a noise like a lorry arriving, and John has

3

to enter and say, "Darling, the new Rolls is a dream!"

There are occasions when it is extremely difficult to decide whether to have the sound or not, but that is where the fun comes in.

In a third class of sounds are those which, whether specified by the playwright or not, assist the atmosphere of the play, such as wind, sea, machinery, and the like. These are of tremendous value, but again must be well done or omitted. A producer who takes trouble over such effects is amply repaid for his efforts, for they act, to some extent, as a compensation for a small stage and indifferent scenery. A wonderful illusion of space can be obtained by arranging sounds of the right pitch and volume, and by paying attention to the balance of foreground noises with those at a distance. It often happens that a producer has no suitable backcloth, and is compelled to cover the deficiency by setting his window in the side-wall of the set. This device does nothing, however, to assist him in his task of conveying to the minds of the audience the locality of the play. Let him study the details of the noises off, therefore. For instance, round a lonely house in open country the wind howls and whistles, but to a house in the woods it is like a roaring roof overhead with the creakings and sighings and flutterings of trees added. The locality of a town house can be indicated very well by the type of sounds audible. Even the size of the house itself, in whatever locality, can be determined by the noise of the front door, or the distance of the bells from the sitting-room.

In these matters producers, who mourn for the

smallness of their theatres, are in reality fortunate, for sounds that will tell the same story to the whole audience in a small hall, will in a big theatre be inaudible to half the audience, or deafening to the other half.

If we are agreed that sound effects are necessary and valuable, the next question to discuss is, what sort of persons are best fitted to produce them? Experimental psychologists divide individuals into two main types, the visual type and the auditory type; those who do the bulk of their observation and memorizing through the senses of sight and hearing respectively. Clearly, an individual of the latter type is required, for he must be able to observe sounds minutely and remember them exactly. He must have a good ear. No one can whistle a tune unless he can **hear it in his brain.** The same is true of sounds of any kind. If a person of the visual type be let loose with a bass drum and a thunder-sheet, he will beat the one and rattle the other, whereas a person of the auditory type will hear a real thunder-storm and reproduce it. The difference in result will be most marked.

Another point of the greatest importance is that, when an effect has been rehearsed and the producer has pronounced it perfect, the effectsman has to be able to remember the exact volume of sound necessary, and that is very difficult, even for the auditory type. Consequently the effectsman must be capable of intense concentration. This refers not to sounds produced by electrical or mechanical means, with which it is always possible to measure and record sound volume, but to those produced vocally, or by muscular action, when it is not possible.

In these cases even the auditory memory is not reliable, for when a man is actually making a noise, a large part of his attention is directed to the process of making it, leaving less to be focused in the sense of hearing. And the louder the noise, the greater must be the difference between two volumes to become perceptible. The ear of a man in the centre of a loud noise is satiated, and becomes incapable of appreciating nice distinctions. Thus then, the ear being handicapped by the lack of attention focused in it, that part of the attention which is directed elsewhere, can be made to furnish compensation. The auditory memory retains its part of the total impression, while the balance is made up by the tactile memory, if we may so call it, the memory that treasures sensations of touch.

For example, a man is required to imitate gunfire by striking a bass drum. To achieve the right volume of sound, he must strike the drum with exactly the right amount of force. He must concentrate, therefore, on that aspect of the matter, the exertion of force. When exerting force, no matter how slight, we can tell how much we have exerted, not in terms of pounds per square inch perhaps, but by the "feel" of it, transmitted to our brains through the sense of touch seated in the joints, muscles, and skin. This "feel" is retained by what I have called the tactile memory. **Let the man rehearse his gunfire, therefore, often enough to impress the correct "feel" on his tactile memory,** and he will be able to experience it in his brain, just as he can hear the sound in his brain. The combined operation of his tactile and auditory memories, each contributing their quota of recol-

6

lection, will then enable him to reproduce the required sound at will.

Producers would do well to grasp this point. Usually they rehearse an effect until it has been done correctly two or three times only and then pass on to something else, forgetting that it is infinitely harder to learn a sensation than to learn dialogue. And again, effects are seldom rehearsed at all until shortly before the first performance, whereas they should be tackled at the beginning and rehearsed as much as the other parts of the play. It may be objected that, because conditions at rehearsal and at performance are very different as a rule, it is better not to practise effects until performance conditions are obtainable, so that the right effect can be gained at once, and the effectsman will not have to unlearn a wrong sensation. But a wrong sensation does form a basis on which to found a right one. Our gunfire man, finding that at rehearsal he has been making less sound than is needed, when the scenery has been interposed between him and the audience, having learnt a wrong sensation, can easily increase his sound proportionately. His wrong sensation forms a standard of comparison. But if he has no chance to try, until the scenery is up, which with costumes, make-up, lighting and properties will be harassing the mind of the producer, he will clearly have insufficient attention paid to his efforts, and will only get comfortable and sure in his job by the time the show is due to come off. And the Press and notables come on the first night.

An effectsman, then, must have a good ear, the ability to concentrate, and he must be sensitive. Yet another indispensable quality is a well-developed sense of rhythm. Suppose that a person is engaged in making sounds to suggest running machinery. He must be able to select the rhythm of the particular machine he is imitating, and stick to it for any length of time without hastening or slackening the pace. With more complicated machinery it may be necessary to have three people engaged, A working at a slow speed, B at a speed twice as fast as A's, and C at a speed that bears no obvious relation to either. A and B must be able to work together, and C must be able to shut his ears to A and B, and stick to his own speed with absolute precision. Any divergence from their given speeds will ruin the effect, since regularity is the essence of machine sounds.

Suppose, further, that the play comes to its climax when the machinery gets out of control and gathers speed, until it jams from overheating. Each of the three will have to increase their speeds, while retaining the same inter-relationship. Poor C!

Under the heading of rhythm-sense the ability to judge intervals between the components of complex sounds must be placed. And it is most important that an effectsman should have this ability, since it is often the correct spacing of the components that gives to the complex sound the characteristics whereby it is recognized, the falsifying of which will render the sound unidentifiable. Or another fault may be made. Though the relative intervals between the components are correct, and the total sound is recognizable, the entire combination may be speeded up, or slowed down, giving the wrong emotional value for its context. A complex sound, supposed to be made off-stage by a character, must have the emotional value of that character at that moment. Undue speed may suggest haste or anger at a moment when laziness or indifference is required, and vice versa. From this we learn that an effects-man, besides having rhythm-sense, must also be something of an actor, since he has to be able to assume, if only momentarily, the mood of any character.

And this fact leads us on to the consideration of how much stage sense is necessary. We may define "stage sense" as "the knowledge of what is drama-tically effective". This knowledge may come either intuitively or by experience, but, clearly, the more of it an effectsman has the better, as a general prin-ciple. More particularly, cases often occur when he has to exercise dramatic judgment. He has to choose the psychological moment for his noise, and make his noise before the moment gets away. One very frequent example of this is when the word-cue for an effect gets a laugh. And as the length of laughs vary with every audience, the effectsman has to judge the laugh at every performance, in order to select his moment. If he functions too soon, the noise of the laugh will kill his effect; if too late, there will be an undramatic pause, during which the play will be "dropped on the floor".

More difficult problems arise sometimes in serious plays, when degrees and durations of emotional ten-sion have to be judged. It will help a player enor-mously to hear a sound, to which he has to react, at the exact moment that he is emotionally ready for it. To do this an effectsman must be able to put himself in tune with the player. He needs for such occasions, and indeed for the whole business, great sympathy, using the word in its true meaning, sympathy not only with his fellow men, as men and as the characters they are portraying, but with all nature. He is producing sounds representing those made by various forces; he should be able to assume, at any rate in part, the nature of those forces, just as a player tries to assume the nature of the part he is playing. So far as the player succeeds in taking on the mentality of his rôle, just so far does he succeed in convincing his audience. The same is true of the effectsman. Both jobs are fundamentally of the mind. We direct our bodies from our brains, so that, if we think rightly, the right actions will follow, and the right impression will be created in the minds of the audience. Therefore *Be* a thunder-storm. *Be* the lazy surf. *Be* a galloping horse, tearing down the forest ride with a hero on your back; shrink from the jarring cobbles in the courtyard, and, when the hero thoughtlessly wrenches your mouth in his haste to dismount, stamp and snort with pain. Anything else will be monotonous, if not wrong, and unworthy of an artist.

There is one quality, one key-quality that an effectsman **must have.** Without it all other qualities are as sheep having no shepherd. It is utter, absolute, cosmic reliability. Nothing makes acting such a nerve-wracking occupation as being unable to rely on the effectsman, and there is probably no actor, professional or amateur, who has not suffered from this particular form of torture at some time. We may take it, therefore, that agreement on this point is unanimous. An actor, who is late for an entrance, has at least to appear and face the music; the crime carries its punishment along with it. But a defaulting effectsman puts his fellow performers to public shame, while himself lies hid in anonimity. He should be made to take a curtain call, in chains.

This risk of missed cues is lessened greatly if the effectsman is properly rehearsed. He learns his part in the same way as do the rest of the company. The order of cues and the length of the waits between them sink into his brain and become a unified performance, as opposed to a string of isolated anxieties. As a rule, the stage-manager and the effectsman are one and the same, and it is of the greatest assistance to a stage-manager to be able to rehearse sufficiently, to know his part, so that, even if his prompt copy were lost or destroyed, he could conduct a performance with confidence. **Stage-managerial confidence is the foundation of successful play production.** Too many producers make drastic changes at the last moment, being unwilling, or unable, to do their thinking at the proper time, namely, before the play goes into rehearsal. As a result, unnecessary strain is put upon the stage-manager, whose first night becomes a first nightmare, instead of a calm, straightforward piece of work.

Another useful, though subsidiary, talent for an effectsman is to be "good with his hands". Ability to work in wood, metal, leather, etc., is a great assistance, because he can then make for himself any necessary contraptions, and experiment with them, and alter them, until they are perfect. If he has to have this part of the work done by somebody else, it is often extremely difficult to describe exactly what is wanted. A great deal of time is wasted in explanation and argument, and he is handicapped by lack of knowledge of the possibilities of various materials. But, if he does the work himself, these handicaps are removed together with certain other difficulties. If with infinite patience and labour he has half-completed a contraption, and he then has a very much better idea, he can quietly scrap the one and start on the other, working, if necessary, all night. When another man is making the first contraption, however, it all becomes very difficult, and the effectsman has either to put up with a second best, or go through the whole process of explanation and argument again in circumstances that are much less comfortable.

So then, for a good effectsman we have to find a person of the auditory type, having a sense of rhythm, as much stage sense and experience as possible combined with acting ability, sympathy, and sensitiveness. Add to these utter dependability and handiness with tools, and season the whole mixture with patience and humour. If he is also a singer, a harpsichord-player and a certified plumber, so much the better.

When a company has discovered such a god-like mortal, their only other difficulty will be to resist the temptation to cast him for the leading part and let the noises "go hang".

Assuming that they do resist temptation, we must now proceed to the consideration of what he has to do and how he should set about it.

CHAPTER II

Method

VERY few sound effects, that are called for in a theatre, are simple. The vast majority are composed of a number of simple sounds, either spaced or simultaneous. It is necessary, therefore, to train the auditory observation. As a musician trains his ear in listening to chords, so that he can tell the notes of which they are composed, so the effectsman must practise listening attentively to sounds, so that he can resolve them into their components. Close observation will enable him to analyse a sound mentally. He can then deal with each component in turn, and invent a way of producing it. Take, for example, a cuckoo clock. The strike is usually represented on the stage by a plain "cuckoo", and for that reason sounds thin and unconvincing even to people not very familiar with them. A great deal more happens really. There is a steady tick-tuck all the time, and a whirr of mechanism during the strike. The strike itself is a blow of a small hammer on a wound spring as well as the "cuckoo", and finally comes the flap of the little door closing. Such an effect would be easy to work, if a real cuckoo clock can be borrowed, in spite of the fact that dramatic time and real time seldom coincide. There is a short string on a cuckoo clock, which, when pulled, makes the cuckoo perform. This is necessary, in order that it may be possible to set the cuckoo at the right time. For theatre purposes all that has to be done is to set the clock going on the stage, having painted the hands to make them indistinct. The cuckoo is set for the required hour, and a string, tied to the short string on the clock, is passed through a hole in the scenery. This string can then be pulled at cue. All the sounds will be genuine, and even the cuckoo weight will descend in view of the audience. If no proper clock can be borrowed, the effectsman has to invent ways of making all the sounds, and perhaps of making the visible mechanism work as well.

This example is rather fussy for practical purposes, but serves to illustrate the principle. A door-slam will be a better example, because it occurs so often, and is so often done wrongly. The old method was to screw a screw-eye into one end of a piece of board or batten about four feet long, and to tie a length of cord to the screw-eye. This device is worked by placing the batten on the stage in a line with the operator's foot with the screw-eye at the end farthest from him. He then places his foot on the near end, and by pulling the cord lifts the far end, so that the batten makes an angle with the stage. By suddenly releasing the cord, the batten comes down on the stage hard by pressure of the foot. An elementary bang is thus produced, bearing little resemblance to the sound of a door shutting, which always has at least one latch, and, if it is a front door, may have Yale and ordinary latches, two loose bolts, a chain, handle rattle, knocker rattle, letter-box rattle, and hinge-squeak.

Listen then carefully to the real sound and analyse it mentally into its components. If any of the components would be inaudible in the circumstances, in which the sound is heard, discard them and concentrate upon those that will tell.

Next comes invention of means to produce the sounds, but clearly there can be no hard and fast rules about this, as it is entirely a matter of particular application. What will serve in one theatre will be inadequate in another. The best that can be done is to suggest possible fields of exploration, and that I have done in later chapters dealing with particular effects.

The methods of producing sounds may be discussed under five headings.

(1) *Actual Sounds*. If the actual sound can be made with the actual thing, or things, that make it, obviously one makes the sound in this way. It saves a lot of bother, and is very uninteresting.

(2) *Gramophone Records*. A very wide range of effects records are obtainable, but there are severe limitations to this method of having the work done. The very means of recording and reproduction distort the majority of sounds, until they are no longer true, giving them a metallic quality. Nowadays most people are familiar with this fact from their experience of broadcasting and the talkies. I remember seeing a chambermaid making a bed in one film, and when she smacked the pillow, it sounded like a tin can. The audience laughed. As a general rule records are completely successful only when the sounds recorded are metallic, e.g. car and airplane sounds.

The records are double-sided and have a series

of effects on each side, usually three, but sometimes five or six. Between the zones of each effect a ring of smooth surface a quarter of an inch wide is left, making it possible to pick out the effect required. This is naturally essential, but it means in practice that the records of continuous effects, such as wind and crowd noises, are of very short duration. Therefore, either two gramophones must be used in turn, in order that the effect may be sustained without a break, or a radiogram is necessary, the volume-control of which makes it possible to "fade" the effect in and out, thereby overcoming the abruptness of the break, while the needle is put back to the beginning.

Ideally, a radiogram should always be used, firstly, because of the vastly better control possible with it; secondly, because it emits a much greater volume of sound than a gramophone, and, thirdly, because, giving this greater volume, the instrument can be placed farther from the stage, so that needle-scratch and other sounds incidental to its operation cannot be heard by the audience.

To a small society, whose financial resources are limited, the hire of a radiogram is a consideration, and the purchase of a record (present price 4s.) for one effect, when the other five may never be used, is another. Also, in a small hall, where off-stage space is cramped, the bulk of a radiogram must not be neglected. Hence it will be seen that gramophone effects are not always so good as would appear at first sight, and though records are the best and cheapest way of producing certain complicated effects, the pros and cons should be carefully weighed before deciding on their general use.

Finally, if the decision is in favour of them, no record should be bought unheard.

A licence for their public performance must be obtained from Phonographic Performance, Ltd., 144 Wigmore Street, London, W.1.

(3) *Electrical—Mechanical.* Electrical and mechanical means are employed principally to produce mechanical sounds, though other sounds can also be made with them, e.g. wind. This heading covers all means of producing sound where the motive force is other than muscular. Strictly speaking, gramophone records should be placed under this heading also, but they are of sufficient distinction and importance to deserve a heading to themselves. For the opposite reason, though neither electrical nor mechanical, compressed air is mentioned here. For certain effects compressed air is indispensable, but they are few.

(4) *Vocal.* Vocal mimicry of all sorts, including whistling, is an invaluable talent for an effectsman to possess. By this one method animals, birds, cars, airplanes, motor-cycles, motor-boats, train sounds, musical instruments, and a host of other sounds can be imitated. The two main difficulties to be overcome are insufficiency of breath to sustain an effect, and the discovery of suitable means of amplification, when necessary.

(5) *Muscular.* This is the most important method, since it is the most used. It is also the most difficult, because, as stated in the previous chapter, there is no way of measuring the amount of force that is being used, and therefore of guaranteeing that an effect will be exactly the same each time it is made. This method demands more skill and concentration

than any other, for in vocal mimicry concentration is focused only in the vocal organs, while the muscular method often calls for the use of several parts of the body at once, and for swift changes from one activity to another both in time and space. This method overlaps the first, in that many actual sounds are produced by the exertion of muscular force, and when many actual sounds have to be made together or in rapid succession, the use of several limbs at once and the swift changes in activity occur just as in making imitative sounds.

These muscular effects are the most pleasing to work. Apart from the benefits that their successful performance brings to the play, the effectsman himself gets tremendous personal satisfaction. He experiences as great a thrill from producing a nicely-timed sound sequence as from performing a piece of music well, or holing a long putt. And being the prime mover of a storm at sea is most exhilarating.

As dependability is the key-quality of an effectsman, so is it also of effects apparatus. Whatever its kind, it must respond reliably according to its nature. It must be accurately controllable. A bearable second best is preferable to a temperamental "beauty". The same remark holds good of actresses. Though a certain apparatus is slow in starting, it may well be used, provided its sloth is constant. The effectsman merely finds out how long elapses between the first motion and the actual start of the effect, and anticipates the cue accordingly. Should this length of time vary, however, he may come in on his cue correctly only once in ten times. Equally, of course, an effect must stop reliably. And, when it is borne in mind upon what slender foundations a dramatic performance rests, it will be readily seen that every conceivable risk must be eliminated.

Actual control of apparatus is vital, therefore. But there is another aspect of the problem of control which is equally important, namely, that of giving cues to an effectsman working in such a position that he cannot hear or see them himself. Sufficient rehearsal will eliminate most risks, because both the giver and receiver of the cue signal will get accustomed to the needs of the case, and the form of signal will become standardized with practice, thereby removing uncertainty. The feeling of helplessness is ghastly, when, launched on a performance, at which you have offered to work an effect, the realization suddenly dawns upon you that you do not know the cue. While running to the stage-manager to ask, you either miss it, or, by distracting his attention, interfere with something that he should be doing.

Even after plenty of rehearsal difficulties may arise at performance, unless proper foresight is used. **It is necessary that the stage-manager should visualize beforehand the off-stage working of the show.** As rehearsals proceed and he gradually learns the requirements, he should piece together in his mind a picture of what will happen. By this means he will save himself an infinity of trouble in all departments of his work, and as regards sound effects he will not find himself trying to give a carefully rehearsed cue to someone invisible behind scenery or lost in a stage black-out.

There are three principal methods of giving cues off-stage: (*a*) by gesture, (*b*) by light, (*c*) by sound.

(*a*) First the stage-manager tells the effectsman

19

to "stand-by", and he then takes up his position with his apparatus. A short time before the cue the stage-manager raises his arm as a "warning". At the cue he brings his arm smartly down to signify "Go". The latter movement must be definite and clear-cut, so that there shall be no chance of it being confused with some other gesture. It may be that while the stage-manager is listening hard for a cue from the stage, another person in the wings starts talking or making a noise, and the stage-manager flaps at him irritably to quell him. Such a gesture might be mistaken by the effectsman, unless the correct "go" gesture is of a kind that would not be made casually, or is accompanied by a look. In any case the stage-manager must be on his guard against being betrayed into some unwise word or action.

Upon occasions, when the effectsman needs to look at what he is to do, the cue by gesture must be anticipated to allow him time to transfer his gaze from it to the apparatus. Or, if another person is available, he can stand with the effectsman and watch the cue for him, passing it on by word or touch.

Cues are often signalled round corners by this method of having relay stations of one or more persons, but they must all be reliable, for if the attention of one is wandering, the method fails.

(*b*) Giving cues by light is the best method, for it is instantaneous, and there are none of the risks of the gesture method. The ideal arrangement is to have two lamps at the prompt corner and two at the effectsman's position, one red and one white at each place. They are connected to two-way switches at each place also, so that when the stage-manager switches on the RED for "stand-by", both red lamps go on, and the effectsman can switch them both off to let the stage-manager know that he is ready. If the red does not go off, the stage-manager has time to investigate the whereabouts of the erring one. All being ready, the stage-manager switches on RED again for "warning", and finally WHITE for "Go". For an effect which needs a cue to start and another to stop, the WHITE is switched on for "Go", left on, and switched off for "stop".

The refinement of double-switching can be dispensed with, provided the effectsman is trustworthy, but it is an advantage to have lamps at the stage-manager's end anyway, because if they do not go on, he knows at once that the system has broken down, and can make other arrangements before it is too late.

In a system in which only one lamp is used, at the effectsman's end, so long as the signals are carefully thought out and agreed upon, there should be no difficulty. Suppose that an effect of long duration is to be worked, and that it is necessary for the volume of sound to increase and decrease at various cues, a system such as the following might be used.

Flicker	=	Warning
On	=	Go
Flicker-On	=	Crescendo
Flicker-Off	=	Diminuendo
On-Off	=	Stop

When a number of short effects follow one another in rapid succession, it is best to have one "warning" at the beginning of the sequence and only "Go" lights afterwards. Intermediate "warnings" will merely harass and confuse both parties.

It is wise to have an alternative system of giving cues arranged, just in case the light fails. Electric lamps have a way of passing out at crucial moments.

(c) Cue-ing by bell or buzzer works on the same principle as by light, but is less satisfactory. In quiet moments the bell may be heard on the stage or in the auditorium, causing distraction. And, if it is toned down to prevent this, noisy moments on the stage or accidental noise off-stage may make it inaudible to the effectsman.

It may be of assistance to discuss the giving of cues to musicians at this point. When giving a cue by gesture, give the "stand-by" some ten lines before the cue. Two lines before the cue give the "warning" by raising the hand or finger. Three or four words before the cue, give the "Go" by one upward and one downward beat of the hand. If only a downward beat is given the players will find it difficult to start together, because certain instruments take longer to get going than others.

In giving cues by light, put RED on ten lines early. The musicians pick up their instruments and put their music in order. One line early switch RED off. The musicians raise their instruments. Three or four words early, switch WHITE on. The musicians draw breath and tense themselves, while the conductor beats time. And so they all come in together on the cue. Exactly the same procedure is adopted in giving cues to single instruments, except that the amount of anticipation of the "Go" varies slightly for different instruments. Horns take considerably longer to sound than trumpets, for instance.

When using bell or buzzer, it is inconvenient to have to ring so many times, so the best plan is to disregard the "stand-by" and give the "warning" four lines early and the "Go" with sufficient anticipation for the instrument in question. This is not so comfortable for the musicians, but serves its purpose.

There is one other method of relaying cues, which is seldom used, being risky, but it has one application worthy of mention. The method is that of using a string from cue-giver to effectsman. The particular occasion, on which it can be used, is when a character, who is not a pianist, has to appear to play on the stage. The string is tied at one end to the music-rest of the piano on stage, passed through a hole in the scenery, and fastened to the wrist of the actual player off-stage. For other purposes the method is too fraught with peril. On one occasion I was in solitary confinement in a very hot stoke-hole with a thunder-sheet for company being part of an earthquake. My cue was to be given by a cord, which led up out of the stokehole, along out of doors, in at the stagedoor, along a passage, and upstairs at right angles to the stage level. Needless to say, everyone passing tripped over the cord, and certain mischievous and vexatious persons from the mews outside gave it a tug now and then, so that by the time the real cue came, I was in a state of exhaustion from premature efforts, and the rest of the theatre personnel were in hysterics.

This is an extreme case, but shows that in effects work, as in everything else, a little plain common sense should be used. In the words of the late Bob Barron, sometime master carpenter of the Theatre Royal, York, "Ee, lad, 'aave a bit o' goomption!"

CHAPTER III

Household Sounds

AS previously indicated, household sounds should be made with reference to the house in which they are supposed to occur. In a small Victorian house full of furniture and draperies, the sounds should be deadened. In a castle a hollow echo will help the illusion.

Let us now consider particular sounds.

(1) *Door-slam.* The old device of a batten slammed on the stage is not good enough. If there is a door off-stage **in the right direction,** clearly it should be used. If not, a dummy door should be made and hung in a box frame (Fig. 1). The frame should be as deep as conveniently possible, for the deeper the frame, the deeper is the sound made by the door closing, and the more firmly will the whole thing stand. Its total bulk must be governed by the off-stage space in the theatre, and it must not be made so large and heavy that it cannot easily be moved, for it may be necessary to set it in various places during the performance. Old doors can often be obtained cheaply from builders.

Differences in the sound can be made by altering the position in which the door-slam is set, e.g. with the open side of the frame against a wall, or facing the audience. Its possibilities can soon be discovered by experiment. The door should be furnished with ordinary handles and lock for general purposes.

Should a full-size door be too bulky for the stage

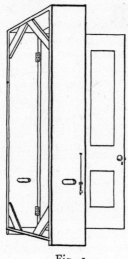

Fig. 1

space available, a much smaller one can be used, set in a deeper frame (Fig. 2).

For the slam of a glazed door, a picture frame containing only the glass might be screwed to the door. I have not tested this idea, but it should work.

(2) *Key and Lock*. The sound of a lock should never be made in mid-air. Always fix the lock to some resonant structure. If you have a door-slam as described above, a lock should be one of its per-

manent fittings. Fasten the key to the frame with a string. A Yale lock can also be fitted permanently, and the latch of it can be fixed back, when the door-slam represents an inside door, and released when a front-door sound is wanted.

For large-lock effects it is better to use an actual lock, if one can be obtained, of the kind used on yard gates and garage doors. Representative sounds can of course be made, but the mixed squeak and

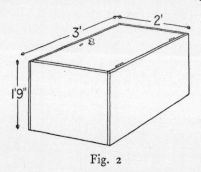

Fig. 2

grate of an elderly dungeon lock, which gives such good atmosphere, is very hard to produce by other than actual means.

(3) *Bolt and Chain*. A bolt and chain can also be screwed to the door-slam for ordinary purposes.

Fortunately for larger bolts, such as are used on iron gates, dungeon doors and the like, it is fairly easy to make imitative noises, otherwise actual means would have to be employed, which would involve borrowing the ducal park gates and conveying them to the theatre, an embarrassing proceeding. The local scrap-iron yard will provide the necessary implements. Two rusty iron bars, one bar and an iron plate, or a cold chisel, a piece of iron pipe and a brick will do, if properly manipulated. The effects-man must be able to visualize the bolt he is imitating, however, and know how it works, before he can hear the sound and imitate it. It may slot into a stone threshold, or pass through a slit in the other gate. In the first case the impact must be solid, metal on stone, and in the second much higher pitched, metal on metal. "Zunk!" and "Cling!" respectively. In both cases the metal used to represent the gate must be fixed, not held in the air, or there will be no resonance, no sense of weight.

For dungeon-door bolts, use metal sliding on wood with a stone impact. The prevalent practice of dropping a handful of chains on to the stage is quite unimaginative and sounds exactly what it is.

(4) *Knocks.* Here the door-slam proves useful again. For front-door knocker effects, a knocker can be fixed to the door, and, if the knocking is supposed to be heard from inside, the door can be set with the knocker on the far side from the audience, so that it comes through the door, as it should. Similarly, if the knocking is supposed to be heard from outside, as in a garden or street scene, the door can be reversed.

When heavy knocking at a castle gate is to be represented, pounding on the stage with a hammer or block of wood is not very effective. Almost all doors rattle when pounded heavily. Stages do not rattle. Our door-slam will be useful again here, beaten perhaps with a padded mallet, if the effect is to be fairly distant. A knocker or a loose bolt fixed on will help to give more rattle.

Upon occasions, when a character knocks at the door of the set, the door-slam should again be used, or a packing-case, or indeed anything yielding the right sound rather than the actual door of the scene. It is such a pity, if the pictures suddenly become animated.

Knocking supposed to be made on the other side of the wall of the set is sometimes difficult to do. There may be no brick wall close enough to the spot from which the knocking should come. It may help to experiment with a large book. Books have a

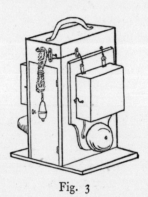

Fig. 3

resonance of their own, which is quite unlike that of wood, but very near that of masonry.

(5) *Door-bell*. The kind of door-bell that is fastened to the door itself with the push outside and the bell inside has a tell-tale sound, and should only be used when it is in keeping with the set and characters. It also can be fitted to the door-slam. A well-made door-slam is certainly a worthwhile investment.

In more genteel houses an electric bell is usual. A piece of equipment kept in most professional theatres is a stout box large enough to contain two dry-cell batteries, having two electric bells screwed to opposite sides and wired to the cells with a push in circuit with each bell. The box has a firm base-board and a handle at the top (Fig. 3). The bells are of different tones, so that one may be used as a telephone-bell and the other as a door-bell. And should one bell give up the ghost, there is the other as an understudy.

As with lock and bolts, bells should not be worked in mid-air, but should be placed on a table or the stage to give resonance and a sense of being fixed. The weight of the bell-box helps in this, while still being easily movable, as every piece of theatrical apparatus should be. It is wise, too, to have pear-shaped pushes on long flexes instead of the ordinary round kind, for it often happens that the stage-manager has to watch his cue through a peep-hole, sometimes in awkward positions. With a long flex he can leave the bell-box standing, as it should, and only has to carry the push.

The old-fashioned wire-pulled bell should be held by that end of its spring which is normally attached to the wall-fitting. A single jerk of the wrist will then cause it to ring in just the right way. If held close to the bell, skill and concentration are necessary, and these are wasted, since the spring will do the work correctly every time.

(6) *Telephone-bell.* Care should be taken in ringing telephone-bells to use the correct method of ringing for the locality in which the play takes place. In London the ring is Burr-burr, 1, 2, Burr-burr, 1, 2, Burr-burr, until the receiver is lifted. In some country places a short ring lasting for a count of three is given first, followed by a pause. Then, if

the receiver is not lifted, a much longer ring is given. On party lines in the country, where one line serves several houses, the line has its own number and each house a subsidiary number. The bell rings the same number of times as the subsidiary number of the house being called, in all the houses.

On most telephones the bell goes "ting" when the receiver is lifted or replaced, and to make this sound every time a stage telephone is used, adds to the illusion quite remarkably.

(7) *Clock-strike*. If the clock is to be set on stage, the actual one that will be used should be inspected before a strike is procured for it, so that the two may match. Though some large clocks have a high-pitched strike in actual fact, too great a disparity between the size of the clock and the note of its strike becomes especially noticeable on the stage. It strikes a false note. Should no suitable bell be available, a triangle will serve, or one of those toy xylophones made with brass strips or tubes, or even a length of steel bar hung up.

No bell or other kind of strike should ever be "damped." It must be allowed to finish vibrating.

(8) *Glass-crash*. The usual way of making a glass or crockery crash is to pour a quantity of broken glass from one vessel to another, and the quantity of glass and vessels used are chosen according to the amount and kind of noise needed. For instance, when in farce someone falls through a greenhouse roof, use two large buckets and a bucketful of glass. When a wooden tray of crockery is dropped on a stone floor, a shallow wooden box should be used, filled with rather more crockery than is supposed to be dropped (that is, if the loaded tray has been seen

30

by the audience), and the crockery should be poured into a wooden packing-case with a slab of stone or slate at the bottom. I advise using more broken material than the supposed smash would yield, especially in small breakages, to ensure that the sound carries, but of course the smash must match the amount smashed to the audience. Only in farce is exaggeration permissible.

In arranging the effect of the breaking of a window-pane, consideration must be given to the following points, namely, whether the pane is broken from inside or outside, the distance from the pane to the surface upon which the broken pieces will fall, and the nature of that surface. When a missile breaks the window of the set and comes into sight of the audience, there is first the impact, followed a moment later by the fall of glass and, simultaneously, the arrival of the missile into sight. This effect can be worked by two people, one to make the impact and one to throw the missile and a handful of broken glass through the window. But if it is inconvenient to have a mess of glass on the stage, the fall of glass must be done off-stage on the same surface as that under the window.

When a missile is thrown through the window from the stage, the impact has to be nicely timed with the thrower's action, and the fall of glass follows after a pause long enough for the broken pieces to reach the ground. Someone must also stand by to catch the missile, so that it makes no untoward noise off-stage. All this seems painfully obvious when set down in print, but mistakes are so often made, that it is wiser to do so.

The best way to produce the impact is to place a

stout picture-frame, with glass firmly fixed in it, over the open top of a box, and to break the glass with a hammer, so that the glass falls into the box. A cheaper method is to break a bottle in the same way. When the fall of glass should follow the impact after a pause, the impact box should be padded, so that the actual fall is silent. The effect fall can then be made in another box, having the right surface ready in the bottom of it. In this way the two halves of the effect are isolated, and any required pause can be made between them.

Squeaks, creaks, and footsteps, though they do occur in houses, are of more general application, and therefore I have dealt with them in Chapter VIII, under the heading of Miscellaneous Sounds.

CHAPTER IV

Machine Sounds

MOST of the effects discussed in the last chapter were produced by using the actual sounds. In this chapter we have to consider effects which must be produced by imitative methods.

(1) (a) *Motor-Car*. An excellent gramophone record is obtainable of car sounds (H.M.V. E574); of starting the engine and driving away; of driving up and stopping; of the engine running continuously, etc. When these effects suit the requirements of the play, they are perfect, but they have this one limitation. Though they can be shortened by "fading out", they cannot be lengthened. As is the case with all records, one must take what the record gives.

For special cases, therefore, some other device must be employed. Electrical car effects are let out on hire by firms dealing with stage lighting equipment, e.g. The Strand Electric Engineering Company. These are composed of an ancient sewing-machine driven by an electric motor. To the motor's fly-wheel two or three short lengths of leather strap are fastened at equal distances from each other. They are attached by one end, leaving their free ends to stand out from the circumference of the wheel like blades of an electric fan. They are of equal length and long enough to slap the base-board as they go round. As the wheel rotates, therefore, a rhythmic tapping sound is produced at low speed, which becomes a continuous purr at high speed. The whole device is mounted in a wooden case with a lid for protection, but there is a hole cut in the side of it covered with perforated sheet metal to allow passage for the sound. Upon the outside of the box a dimmer is fixed, which is connected in circuit with the motor and controls its speed. The hum of the motor, the tapping of the straps, and the sounds of the sewing-machine combine to make a very efficient car effect, and the box, in which they are contained, gives resonance and helps to mix the unitary sounds together. It is very difficult to achieve the sharp break, and re-start at another note, occasioned by a change of gear, because the electric motor will not stop dead and start again at a high speed, but in these days of easy gear-change, the defect is not so noticeable. The procedure for representing a car moving off from a standstill is as follows. Advance the dimmer a little. The motor begins to rotate slowly. The car is at rest, ticking over. Advance the dimmer rapidly for a count of six. The car moves off in bottom gear, making a good deal of noise. Retard the dimmer sharply as far as it will go, cutting off the current. The motor loses speed quickly, and the sound drops in tone. The car is now moving with the clutch out, its engine losing speed, while the gear is being changed. Advance the dimmer more slowly, i.e. to the same place, but during a count of ten. The car gathers speed in second gear. Retard the dimmer as before, for the change up into top gear, let the motor lose speed, and advance the dimmer very slowly again, so that the car moves along with quite a low purr. To make the car pass out of hearing, slowly cover the open side of the box with a padded board, and then slowly retard the dimmer to stop the motor.

For changing down the procedure is reversed. When the clutch is slipped for the change, advance the dimmer sharply, in order to "rev. the engine up", and retard it, when the clutch is let in.

If the occasion does not warrant the hire of such an elaborate contraption, a sewing-machine alone with straps lashed to its fly-wheel, and covered with a resonating hood, can be made to give good results, especially if the operator adds something vocally.

In a small hall vocal noises alone can be very effective. A reasonably good car can be imitated to perfection by a male voice, especially if the noises are made into a bedroom jug. An old car makes too much rattle to be easily imitated, and it does not as a rule "get away" quickly enough. Because the sound must be made as loudly as possible, a good deal of breath must be used, and a man cannot sustain the sound long enough to copy a slow car, even considering the opportunities for taking breath that the gear-changes afford.

Other sounds can be added, however, to help the illusion. Once in weekly repertory, when time was short, the effect of a charabanc arriving was made by one man. He made the engine sound by growling into a pewter pint mug, the squeak of the brakes by rotating the point of a penknife on a plate, the "prup" of the hand-brake by drawing a screw-driver across a row of partly-driven nails, and the wheels on gravel with two pieces of sand-paper. Actually it was not very satisfactory, but had there been more time for experiment, an intrinsically sound idea could have been perfected.

Parenthetically, another quality needed by an effectsman is control of his sense of humour. The production of some of these effects is irresistibly comic, and even though the effectsman may be doing his work quite calmly, he may suddenly catch the infection from the snorts of the bystanders and ruin all by laughing.

The sound of the self-starter can be made by rubbing a small tin box on an uneven wooden floor with a circular motion. The right tin must be found by experiment, but I have used a rectangular one measuring $4'' \times 3'' \times 1''$, with a hinged lid, which was left open and provided the peculiar tinny clatter of some self-starters.

Before leaving the subject of cars, mention should be made of an excellent record (H.M.V. E578) of fire-engine effects, as follows: English Fire-engine —(a) Bell continuous; (b) Bell intermittent; (c) Fire-engine approaching and receding. American Fire-engine—(a) Fire-bell; (b) Fire-engine; (c) Police patrol.

Finally, where the architecture of the theatre and its surroundings permit, a great deal of trouble can be saved by using an actual car outside.

(b) *Motor-Cycle*. It is a very great blessing if an actual motor-cycle can be used outside, for near effects, because, as far as I have been able to discover, there are no records made, and the thing is so noisy and complex that it is exceedingly difficult to imitate.

The only time I was in a play in which a very near effect was needed, an actual cycle was used on the stage, and the leading man made a somewhat hazardous appearance on it. As a sound effect it was bad, because, of course, it was deafeningly loud, and the cycle was supposed to approach from a distance, which could not actually be managed.

It had to be started with a kick behind the scenery, and to anyone with ears it was perfectly obvious what was being done. However, the play was a farce, and the badness of the effect was not so ruinous as it would have been in some less light-hearted entertainment.

The effect of a distant motor-cycle can be produced vocally with great success, but I must confess that the production of a near effect defeats me. I have never had to achieve one—I was not stage-managing the play to which I have referred—and have never found myself possessed of sufficient desire, money, time, and enthusiasm to tackle the problem from sheer love of learning. No one, I imagine, outside a theatre, would deliberately make that particular noise, unless they wished to go somewhere in a hurry. But if I came across this problem in the course of my work, I should begin to solve it by collecting an electric motor, a dimmer, some pieces of strap and tin, a drum, some iron piping, and the toothed wheel and chain of a pedal cycle. I should screw the motor to a board, and bolt the toothed wheel to its fly-wheel, arranging the chain upon it. At the distance of the chain's length from the motor I should fix a piece of pipe horizontally between two uprights, parallel to the axle of the motor, and having a piece of pipe of slightly larger bore rotating upon it. I should pass the chain over these pipes before fixing them. When the motor drives the chain, it will cause the outer, loose pipe to rotate and rattle on the inner pipe. If it did not make the right tinkling sound, I should try wiring small pieces of tin loosely at intervals along the chain. All this ought to make something like the sound.

Now to the exhaust. I should bolt a coffee-tin to the toothed wheel, having first riveted two or three short lengths of strap to it, and I should mount the board carrying the apparatus on legs long enough to allow the drum to be placed under the straps, so that they would play upon it.

Having reached this stage, I should connect up with the dimmer, plug in, and test. If it was not right, I should search for the fault, and go on "mucking about" until it was right.

If I could not get an electric motor, I should use an old knife-cleaning machine or some other such rotary contrivance as a prime mover.

What I call "mucking about" is scientifically known as "The Method of Trial and Error", the method almost invariably employed in inventing sound-effects apparatus.

(For Back-firing, see Chapter VII.)

(2) *Train*. The records of train effects are H.M.V. E583; (*a*) train stationary; (*b*) train starting; (*c*) train in motion; (*d*) train stopping; (Other side), Underground noises, (*a*) lift sounds; (*b*) Underground train sounds; and Columbia YB6, American train: starting; in motion and stopping. English train: starting; in motion and stopping.

These are very good. I have heard them used on two or three occasions at Drama Festivals with complete success. The only difficulty is to join the effects together, when, for instance, a train is heard arriving, stationary, and starting—a single continuous effect. They are divided on the records, otherwise it would not be possible to time the effect to fit every different length of dialogue. The joining of these divisions must be masked with a foreground of supplementary sounds, such as shouting, talk, luggage noises, etc.

The fourth effect of a train in motion is recorded from outside the train, and is meant for the sound of trains passing on a line near which the scene is laid. It would hardly do for the accompaniment to a scene played in a railway compartment.

These records will be suitable for most needs, and the least expensive method, for clearly the making of imitative sounds is a complicated business. The train effect in "The Ghost Train" at the Garrick Theatre in 1926 was produced with the following apparatus: a garden roller pushed over slats of wood nailed to the stage at regular intervals, to represent the train passing over the rail joints; three cylinders of compressed air, one to blow the whistle, the second for an uninterrupted steam effect, and the third used with a tin, covering and uncovering the jet rhythmically, for the exhaust; a large tank; a large thunder-sheet; a thick, oval thunder-sheet and mallet; a whistle, for distant whistle effect; a side-drum and jazz-drummer's wire brush; another side-drum and a small padded mallet; a bass drum; some heavy chains; and sand-paper for distant puffing effect. Seven men were employed to work it all.

This effect was arranged for a large theatre, and was very good indeed. For a smaller theatre no doubt less apparatus would be needed. The tank and the oval thunder-sheet could be omitted, and the work of the air-cylinders, which cost 7s. 6d. each, could be done with foot-pumps and inflated tyres or camp mattresses. Even so it would be quite a large undertaking requiring considerable space and personnel.

At any rate there is the recipe for a good train effect. The heavy chains were used for the clanking of the connecting-rods. This sound, so characteristic of the locomotive engine, could be made with a good length of deal batten or plank resting loosely in wooden slots. When struck with a padded mallet, it would rattle in just the right way, and is more easily obtained than heavy chains.

The sand-paper for the puffing effect should be arranged in this way. A cylinder (A) of cardboard three feet long and having a diameter of three to four inches, should be lined with coarse sand-paper glued in. A second cylinder (B), of the same length but of slightly smaller diameter, should be covered on the outside with glued sand-paper for half its length, and its sand-papered end should be blocked. This cylinder (B) should fit inside the first (A), so that the two surfaces of sand-paper engage, but not too tightly. By working (B) in and out, the puffing sound is produced, and the note varies with the distance that (B) is pushed into (A), becoming higher and thinner, the farther (B) goes in. This device brings the puffing from the distance, when it is first heard, up to the limit of loudness that the device can produce, at which point the side-drum and wire brush "take over", and bring it right into the station.

(3) *Stationary Machines*. There is not a great deal that can be said of general application on this part of the subject. Everything depends upon the requirements and circumstances of each particular case. The effectsman can merely be advised to pay a visit to the machinery he has to imitate, and analyse and invent for himself. Stationary machinery is a great deal easier to deal with than locomotive. It does at least stay in one place, and the only crescendo that is likely to be needed is when a door opens, letting the sound through. A combination of drums, vacuum-cleaner, sewing-machine, and hammers of different weights, played rhythmically on various surfaces, should provide a good general foundation of sound with which to experiment.

An oil-engine's exhaust can be imitated with a wire brush and a small bass drum. "Swish, thump, swish, swish, thump, swish, thump, thump, swish, swish, swish, etc."

Columbia YB17 records the sounds of a printing press.

(4) *Carts and Carriages*. In the matter of carts and carriages several points must be noted. The kind of vehicle and its size will probably be stated in the text, or at any rate implied, but consideration must also be given to the surface over which it is travelling and its speed. And, further, when a cart is in question, one must inquire whether it is loaded or not, and, if so, the amount and nature of the load. The speed and rumble of an empty carriage will differ from those of a loaded one only very slightly,

41

as told by their sound, but an empty cart travels faster and makes much more rattling and reverberating, than one loaded with soil or hay. A milkfloat, a brewer's dray, and a tumbril all sound distinctly different. Stress cannot be laid too often on this point of the differences of similar sounds, and the need for paying close attention to them. A sound effect must be instantly recognizable, otherwise doubt will occupy the minds of the audience, distracting their attention from the play; or worse, an entirely erroneous impression will be created, which, when it is corrected, will cause amusement or annoyance.

Here again analysis plays a great part. In Gordon Bottomley's play, "Midsummer Eve", a horse-drawn cart loaded with hay is supposed to approach the scene, which represents a barn, and instead of turning into the barn, as the characters expect, it passes across on a road at the back in sight of the audience, and draws up in an imagined yard beyond. In most theatres this would be impossible. It is also, luckily, unnecessary. So, in my production of this play, a sound effect was arranged to give the impression that the cart approached, but just before appearing, turned down beside the barn to a yard on the near side. The effect was simplified as much as possible, because rehearsal time was very short, and the cart sound was made by a rumble with the fingers on a large bass drum punctuated by rhythmic taps on its shell, to represent the sound made by a wheel loose in its axle. The road surface was imagined to be soft enough to be disregarded so far as the cart was concerned. The horse's hooves were made to thud heavily, as on the harder centre of the

road, occasionally striking a stone. Both horse and
cart approached from silence, until the moment
arranged for turning the corner. Then the horse
snorted and broke into a heavy trot for some six
or eight paces, down the imagined incline beside
the barn, the cart naturally rumbling and tapping
faster to match. Both horse and cart then slowed
to a walking pace and faded out by rapid diminuendo of volume. It had been intended to throw a
moving shadow on the opposite side of the barn
entrance at the moment the cart was turning, thrown
supposedly by the setting sun, but, alas, owing to
lack of time this beautiful scheme had to be aban-
doned; nevertheless the sound effect worked most
satisfactorily. The technique of the horse will be
dealt with more fully in Chapter VI, but the success
of the effect depended mainly upon teamwork, and
that was only possible because both "horse" and
"cart" knew in their minds exactly the road they
were to travel.

Quite a good effect of carriage-wheels on cobbles
can be obtained by playing a roll on a very slack
side-drum of the military pattern. An orchestral
side-drum would be too high-pitched, even when
slackened off. The roll must not be played too
expertly, as some unevenness is good. Considered
alone, the effect is only approximately right,
but when the horse-hooves are added, the total
effect is good, and it has this great advantage
over more mechanically made rumbles, that the
volume can be altered at will, and also the tone,
by playing on different parts of the drumhead.
It has the key-quality of being absolutely controllable.

Another similar effect can be produced with bass drumsticks and an empty wooden case. Start softly drumming with two sticks on the inside of the case; increase the noise, then change the method to stirring with one stick, so that it strikes each side in turn. The result will be a hollow rumble suitable for an empty cart or tumbril passing over cobbles.

For the effect of wheels on gravel actual means are best. A wooden trough should be made, say twelve feet long, six inches wide and four inches deep. This should be filled with gravel, carefully graded from coarse at one end down to fine sand at the other. A separate wheel can be run in this, or a wheel-barrow can be pushed along it. The wheel will be practically silent at the sandy end, and the sound will grow as it nears the other end. The operator must wear soft shoes. The horse-hooves can be worked in another smaller gravel box nearby. A motor wheel can be used in the same way.

Another method is to make a wooden drum containing gravel, which is rolled on the stage, though this is not nearly so good, and yet another employs sand-paper, graded from fine to coarse and glued to a board three or four feet in length, upon which a block of wood covered with sand-paper is pushed along. This way is satisfactory in a small hall, and its volume can be increased by using the bottom of a packing-case instead of a board.

(5) *Boats*. Of steamships' engine-rooms I have, alas, all too little experience, but while crossing to Ireland recently I took the opportunity of listening to what was going on around me, before trying to

sleep. I have managed to reproduce the effect quite well, while sitting at the table typing. The table has two drawers, both empty and fairly loose. My typewriter is a Corona Portable and stands on a folded rubber sheet. I wear a signet ring on the little finger of my left hand. By pounding alternately with my closed fists I find that I get a surprisingly good representation, for the table booms, the drawers make one rattle, the typewriter another, and the ring striking through the rubber sheet gives exactly the right knocking sound. I doubt whether one could keep this up for any great length of time, however, but the work of each hand could be given to a separate person, thereby halving the labour.

It is quite possible, indeed probable, that the effect worked in just this way would not be loud enough. In that case substitutes, that give more sound, must be found for each of the ingredients, for instance, a bass drum instead of the table, a tea-chest for the drawers, with a selected assortment of objects upon it, which would dance with the vibration, and perhaps mallet-blows on the end of a stout wooden post in place of the ring-knocking. In any event, where the scene is set aboard ship, the engines are stationary in relation to the scene, and must be dealt with on the same principle as stationary machines.

In plays such as "Outward Bound" and "Pleasure Cruise", in which the engine-room is far removed from that part of the ship represented on the stage, a large electric fan gives a faint hum, which creates, as it were, a "feeling" of engines somewhere, and, if there is a door leading to the deck, the air-flow can be directed effectively on to the characters as they pass through.

Suppose that the scene was set in a dockside warehouse, and the effect of a ship docking or sailing were required, then the ship's engines, which would be running slowly, could be disregarded, or rendered by a low murmur, which the many other sounds of water, donkey engines, sirens and whatnot would practically drown.

The essential sounds of a donkey engine are a continuous singing of metal and a rhythmic "ting-ting-ting", both of which vary considerably in note and speed with the rapidly altering strains put upon the engine. A rotary contraption could, no doubt, be made to produce these sounds, but I think that it could be done by hand equally well, if not better, by playing a drum-roll with metal rods on an anvil, or some large chunk of metal. By this latter method it would be easier to fade the effect out.

Motor-boat effects are rather difficult, and there are no records of them to be had. The "put-put-put" of the submerged exhaust seems to be a unique sound. I succeeded in producing it once, in a small theatre, by striking obliquely with my thumb-knuckle the head of a small gong-drum through thin material loosely draped over it. The material partly muffled the drum and under the glancing blows added a helpful "zip-zip" sound to the total. But, naturally, only a slow boat can be copied in this way. A speed-boat is out of the question, unless one cared to risk an attack of St. Vitus's dance.

However, it might be possible to achieve speed by substituting an electric motor with strap-ends, as described in the section on car effects, for the thumb-knuckle. Indeed, The Strand Electric Engineering Company hire out such a device as an airplane effect, in which the strap-ends play directly on the drumhead. If material were introduced between them, there seems to be no good reason why a speedboat should not result.

While investigating squeaks and creaks for Chapter VIII I discovered another possibility for a motor-boat effect, contrived with a coffee-tin and a piece of string. I removed the lid of the tin, punched a hole in the centre of the bottom of it, and passed the string through, knotting it on the inside. I held the tin at the bottom, with the finger and thumb of my left hand, and placed my right foot on the end of the string to hold it taut. When I tapped the string with my right hand, a "pock-pock-pock" resulted, very suggestive of a motor-boat.

Releasing compressed air beneath the surface of a tank of water presents itself as another splendidly sloppy field of exploration. Again an inflated camp mattress might be pressed into the service, and a pleasant picture is conjured up of the effectsman, supine and at his ease, simultaneously playing the parts of the Captain, the cook, and the bosun's mate in various voices.

(For other nautical noises see Chapter VIII, Section 7, Creaks and Squeaks, and Section 8, Halyards.)

(6) *Airplanes*. Here again excellent records are obtainable of an airplane taking off, landing, zooming, and in continuous flight. (H.M.V. E581, Columbia YB5.)

The effect mentioned in the previous section is a second alternative, and in a small hall vocal imitation by two people working in turn through tin megaphones is successful. But the records are the best method.

(7) *Agricultural Machinery*. I expect that the majority of my readers will be far more conversant with these sounds than I am, but for the sake of those who live in towns, I feel that I must not shirk the subject. Fortunately agricultural sounds are easy to produce. They are mostly clackety and rattling, suggesting the works of Heath Robinson. I have listened closely to two reapers mowing hay, and produced a fair imitation by drawing figures of eight with a short stick on a stretch of wire-netting. A deeper note creeps in as a reaper comes nearer, and this could be done by rapid strokes with tympani-sticks on a biscuit tin, but it must be done very lightly, as the deeper note is not at all marked. Heard from inside a house, the sound is like that of a lawn-mower of the smallest kind. An important point in imitating reapers, that might escape the unwary, is this, that the work does not proceed continuously, but the machine is frequently stopped to clear the blades and to turn corners. At each stop the labourer's "woa" and "gi-up" are heard, sometimes so close together, that one marvels at the intelligence of the horses.

A threshing-machine makes a continuous humming not unlike a distant airplane. This had best be done vocally by emitting a continuous sound, but changing it by opening and closing the mouth and by using different vowel sounds, thus: um . . . ah . . . or . . . ee . . . um . . . or . . . um, and so on.

These two machines are the only ones likely to occur in plays, but if others should be required, I can only repeat my advice, that the effectsman listens to them for himself, for even were I thoroughly familiar with them, I doubt whether a verbal description would be of any service.

CHAPTER V

Nature Sounds

(1) *Wind*. The most frequently used of nature sounds in plays is that of the wind. It has a splendid atmospheric effect, and it is worth while therefore to take great pains to find a good way of producing it. The records of the real thing, though good as far as reproduction goes, are not very serviceable. Firstly, they do not last long enough, so that, although with a radiogram the breaks can be smoothed over, the violence of the storm continually dies away to nothing **at regular intervals.** Secondly, in a long scene with many repetitions of the record the audience are apt to become familiar with it, and each repetition becomes more ludicrous. Thirdly, the record gives only what is recorded upon it, and consequently it is by sheer luck alone that crescendos come at effective moments. It is true that an efficient effectsman can overcome most of these difficulties by skilful manipulation of the volume-control, but, when any kind of wind-machine is used, the difficulties do not arise. A wind-machine is an **instrument** upon which the sensitive effectsman can play any required tune, and, moreover, "accompany" a scene in the most telling manner.

By far the best kind is the electric motor that has lengths of drain-cane fixed to radiate from its fly-wheel, usually four in number. This is housed in a box having one side open, save for a protective screen of wire-netting, and is controlled by a dimmer. The whirling canes make a real sound of wind, undistorted by reproduction, and under absolute control.

An ingenious person could, no doubt, adapt an electric fan to this purpose.

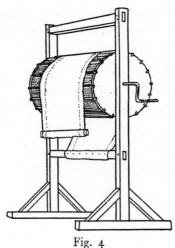

Fig. 4

The other type of wind-machine, widely used in the theatrical world and dating from before the days of electricity, is also effective. It consists of a wooden drum, composed of two circles of wood connected by strips, the outer corners of which have been chamfered. The drum is mounted to rotate on a wooden stand, and a strip of sail-canvas is stretched over it. A handle is fitted to the end of the drum's axle (Fig. 4). When the drum is turned, the chamfered strips rub the canvas and make it shriek. In the construction of this machine, particular attention should be paid to the joints of the stand and the axle-bearings. Constant and violent use puts great strain on these, so that they work loose in time and add unwanted bumps and squeaks to the sound of wind. It is well to use bolts at the joints, which can be tightened as "play" develops.

But suppose that your records get broken, your electric motor burns out, your wind-machine disintegrates, or is left behind at the store. What is to be done? Collect your mightiest men or women, not less than three in number, and bid them whistle and vocalize—for it cannot be called singing—simultaneously. This is done by pursing the lips for whistling and emitting a sustained "oo" from the throat, the air from which passes through the lips and forms the whistle. The pitch can be altered at will and the result is very creditable wind. One person can sustain the sound for about fifteen seconds, so the performers must function in rotation, overlapping each other. It is better not to try and hold on until all one's breath is used, for this is needlessly exhausting. Each person should hold on only as long as he can in comfort.

(2) *Rain*. The sound of rain can be imitated in several ways also. In the production of the play, "Rain", at the Croydon Greyhound Theatre (now extinct), a perforated pipe was connected to the fire hydrant and suspended outside the veranda of the set. A metal trough was set under it, with a wastepipe leading down through a cut in the stage to the yard behind the theatre. When the tap was turned on, there was genuine rain, and with the addition of

a couple of sun-blinds, some raffia, and a truck-load of aspidistras, it was rain in a South Sea island.

In such a play, with rain playing the title-rôle and, so to speak, on the stage for the greater part of the action, this realistic method is well worth the trouble. The fact of having real rain indoors is a bit of extra fun for the audience, and although it is inclined to distract their attention from the play at first, they soon become accustomed to it and accept it as part of the illusion.

Who was it that said that it was no disadvantage for an effectsman to be a certified plumber? Even a grocer has his merits in this work, for the other rain devices use dried peas or rice, and, if they can be had gratis, so much the better for the production costs.

The most ancient rain effect seems to be the rain-box. This is a closed box some six to eight feet in length and about six inches square in section. Nails are driven into the bottom of it thickly, so that the greater part of their length comes through on the inside. A shovelful of peas are put in and a handle of some kind is fixed to one end. Two of these boxes are necessary for the complete effect, and are mounted and worked as shown in Fig. 5.

This piece of apparatus is effective, but cumbersome, and its uses are limited to rain and sea effects. And even within these limits it is limited again, for it always sounds the same, except in so far as the peas are made to run fast or slowly. Far more can be achieved with peas in a gong-drum, e.g. a bass drum having only one head. For the loud roar of heavy rain on a galvanized-iron roof or for a waterfall, the drum should be suspended head downwards, so that it hangs at a slight slant. For the effectsman's comfort it should hang waist-high. It is worked by imparting a slow spinning motion, like that of a spinning coin just before it comes to rest, so that the peas travel round inside continuously. The drum is hung at a slant to make the peas settle in one place, when the drum is not in motion. A piece of material, e.g. a small blanket, should be kept handy

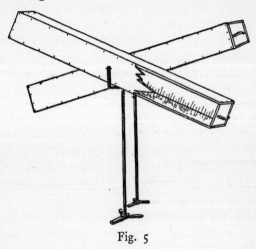

Fig. 5

to stuff in on top of the peas, lest an accidental collision cause a water-spout at an inappropriate moment. Differences can be made in the volume of sound by substituting lead shot or rice for peas, and in pitch by resting the drum on various surfaces; for instance, by laying it flat on a folded blanket to muffle the head. If this is done, the peas must, of course, be stirred by hand.

It will be seen already how invaluable a gong-drum is for all sorts of effects. In one play I used one for sea, oil-engine exhaust, motor-boat engine, and for the sound of the boat grinding against the landing-stage.

Finally, if all else fails, peas in a cardboard hat-box will serve for rain.

(3) *Thunder*. Records of thunder are utterly useless for theatre purposes. They are only endurable in broadcasting or the talkies, when all the audible part of the entertainment is delivered through the same medium.

Of the devices for thunder, the thunder-gallery gives the most faithful rendering. This is a zig-zag channel made of wood and sheet iron with steps and sheer drops in its course, and it is built against the wall of the stage from the grid to the stage level. Cannon-balls are rolled down. It must be most satisfying to the ego to do so. But the cost of its erection is so great, that it is uneconomical, considering the comparatively small use that can be made of it. Also it makes such a tremendous noise, that it would be out of the question in a small theatre. As with records, one must take what it gives. No silencing is possible. To be sure, a pup size might be built, but it is doubtful if its use would justify its bulk.

Next comes the thunder-cart. This is a large wooden case on solid wooden wheels, the circumferences of which are uneven, so that they bump as they revolve. This too is splendid, used in conjunction with a thunder-sheet, but again is bulky and needs clear space in which to travel. If there is space, well and good. If not, the thunder-sheet must be used alone or with a bass drum.

The thunder-sheet should be of fairly heavy-gauge

E

sheet-iron, so that it will stand hard use without becoming dented, and should measure at least six feet by three. To its top edge ∩-shaped loops of metal, round in section, should be riveted firmly, which will neither rattle nor cut the sash-line by which the sheet is suspended. A handle of similar metal should be riveted to the bottom edge. The sheet is then suspended, well clear of obstructions, by a line that passes over a pulley in the roof and

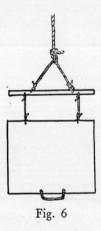

Fig. 6

is made fast to a cleat on the wall, in order that the sheet may be pulled up out of the way when not in use. A piece of batten should be introduced, as shown in Fig. 6, to keep the lines from the ∩-shaped loops apart, otherwise the sheet will cockle down the middle.

A large sheet giving low notes will be sufficient for most purposes, but more realistic effects can be obtained if a bass drum is used as well. Those strings of separate bumps that occur in thunder, like luggage being heaved about overhead, cannot be made on a thunder-sheet, even by beating it with drum-sticks, a practice which is in any case detrimental to it. The drum will supply these, if it is slackened off to kill its musical quality, and given blows at right angles to its head instead of the correct glancing blows of expert bass-drum playing. By this I do not mean to imply that this is the only way to use a drum in thunder effects. Rather I would urge that every possible variety of sound be wrung from it, and in this connection I advise the use of two sticks always, since it is impossible to play a roll with one only.

At the Old Vic we used to make thunder in this way with thunder-sheet, drum, a large galvanized iron tank, and a saucer-shaped splash bath, of the type called "God save the king's", because you have to stand up in them. Once after a rehearsal of the early scenes of "Julius Cæsar", Mr. Harcourt Williams, the producer, was kind enough to say that he had never heard "so musical a discord, such sweet thunder".

(4) *Sea*. For sea, as for rain, the gong-drum and peas are used. The drum should be tilted, one side resting on the floor, the other on some firm object about one foot high. The effectsman kneels facing the lower side (on a cushion, if it is a long cue), and works the peas by hand. By using each hand alternately, a continuous sound can be kept going, while the slope of the drum enables him to make a wave break at any moment. This is done by pushing a handful of peas up round the side, making the noise of a wave coming shorewards, and releasing them at the top, so that they run down across the resonant

centre, making the sound of the wave breaking. Owing to the slope of the drum, the peas soon come to rest at the bottom. If the waves are breaking on sand lazily, a slight silent pause should be left before starting the next wave. But, if the beach is shingle and steeply-pitched, as large a quantity of peas as possible should be taken up for each wave, but only half-way, so that it is louder and shorter, and as the peas come to rest, the top layer of the pile should be drawn over those underneath to make the sound of the water rapidly receding.

When the sea is stormy on a rocky coast, the sound is a continuous roaring, as the waves fall back upon each other. There is no rhythm, but now and again a wave breaks with a "flump" against the rocks and spurts into the air, falling with a splash. So the effectsman should dash the peas about with both hands most of the time, but occasionally let them settle. Just before they do so, he should make the "flump" by thumping the drumhead with the flat of his hand, leave a pause, while the water spurts, then dive his hand into the pile, for the splash.

He should have plenty of peas, at least two pints, and wear stout gloves, if he values his finger-nails.

In a small theatre sea can be imitated with wire brushes on a drum, and the method has this advantage, that the drum can be used instantaneously for another effect, whereas, when peas are used, it must be carried carefully out of earshot and emptied first. But either method is preferable to the use of a rotating wooden cylinder containing peas. Indeed, there is no comparison, for the cylinder will produce lazy surf and rain, but nothing else, with the possible exception of wheels on gravel, while with the drum and peas every kind of water effect is easily accomplished and the drum, as I have said, has a large number of other uses besides.

As well as merely imitating the sea in a realistic manner, the effectsman can make a tremendous emotional effect by adapting the mood of the sea to that of the scene that is being played. He can let the sea be, as it were, an accompaniment to the melody of the voices, interpreting by its volume and rhythm the emotions of the characters. Care must always be taken not to drown an important line by making a wave break at the same moment, but he can make a virtue of necessity. Instead of merely trying to avoid this elementary fault, he can actually stress the importance of the line by treating the wave-break as an accent, and timing it to fall just at the psychological moment.

This principle can be applied equally to wind and thunder, and in a lesser degree to sound effects generally.

It is for work of this kind in particular that a sensitive effectsman is needed. **He has to take part in the scene,** although invisible and with small hope of public recognition. A dull person will be unable to appreciate the difference between a realistic effect and an emotional one, let alone be able to produce it.

(5) *Avalanche.* The word avalanche is here used in its general sense, as a heading that covers earthquake, landslide, falling masonry, and the like; in fact, any event involving the movement of large quantities of solid matter. A shipwreck and a train-smash are closely related to an avalanche in so far as sound effects are concerned, for in these as in

those mentioned above we meet the most difficult problem of all, namely, how to give the impression of great weight falling without damaging the fabric of the theatre and endangering ourselves and others.

A thunder-gallery would be a great asset for such an effect, but they are rare even in the professional theatre, and certainly not worth erecting by amateurs for a few performances only.

The best piece of apparatus known to me is at the Old Vic. It was presented by Miss Edith Evans, for whom it was constructed to represent the collapse of the temple of Dagon in her production of "Delilah". For that reason it is familiarly known as "Edith". It consists of a large cast-iron stand, upon which an octagonal drum rotates. The drum measures some three feet six inches across by one foot six inches thick. The sides are of wood and the barrel of sheet-iron. The sides are joined together with stout pieces of wood screwed on outside the sheet-iron to give added strength. It is fed with cannon-balls through a trapdoor in one side, which, when the drum is turned by hand, rush round and make a splendid crashing, rumbling, grinding noise. Fig. 7 shows "Edith" full face and in profile. It is necessary to ensure that the cannon-balls settle properly after use to prevent them re-arranging themselves noisily at a wrong moment.

Another piece of apparatus, which I have seen in a train accident effect, is made as follows: a piece of heavy-gauge sheet-iron is punched full of ragged holes from one side only, so that it resembles a giant cheese-grater. When dragged across the stage with weights upon it, it makes the noise of railway coaches telescoping. It would seem wise to lay a special floor of rough boards for this effect, though I do not remember that that had been done when I saw the thing in action.

A loud clatter-crash is usually made by simply dropping an armful of stage braces, but there is a better and more controlled way. A number of boards of equal length have holes drilled in them, one at each end, and through these holes ropes are passed and knotted under each board. The two

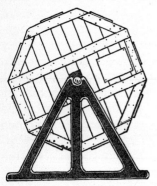

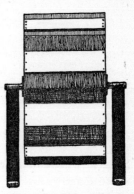

Fig. 7 (Profile)   Fig. 7 (Full-face View)

ropes are tied together to a third rope at the top, which passes up over a pulley and down again. When the whole affair is pulled up, the knots in the two ropes keep the boards a few inches apart from each other, so that they look like the slats of a venetian-blind. This crash can be dropped accurately and, as important, it can be taken up noiselessly afterwards into the overhead space. Braces, when dropped loosely, fly about, cracking ankle-bones, and are noisy to clear up.

With an "Edith", drums, thunder-sheets, etc.,

one can produce a creditable avalanche, which is a continuous rumble, but the practically insoluble problem is how to achieve a single, heavy, climactic thud, such as is needed so greatly in the first scene of "The Tempest", when the ship founders. It could perhaps be done by reinforcing the stage and building a tower of solid timbers up to the fly-floor, down which a really heavy weight could safely be dropped, but I fear that the expense combined with the objections of the owners of the building or of the local Council would rule out such a solution.

(6) *Conflagration*. The ingredient noises of a con-flagration are roaring, hissing, and crackling. The roaring should be made with a wind-machine, prefer-ably an electric one with a large resonating hood over it to amplify its lower notes. Having no efficient wind-machine, it would be interesting to try peas or even a few golf-balls in a drum. I believe that would be successful, especially if it were kept in the background and mixed with the hissing and crackling.

For hissing, escaping air will clearly be best, but sand-paper skilfully manipulated would be a very good second-best.

Loud crackles are produced by drawing a handful of plasterer's lathes rapidly across a grating or the rungs of a ladder. Half a dozen should be held so that their ends project in echelon, the end of the bottom one being nearest the hand. In this way a more continuous sound is obtained—"Ri-i-i-i-ip" instead of "Pat-pat-pat". The medley of lesser crackles are easily made by several people rustling large sheets of brown wrapping-paper. Each sheet should be held at the top and shaken like a thunder-sheet. The smooth, heavy brown paper is the best kind to use, and grease-proof paper is also good, if used with it in the proportion of one to three.

When the fire is a bonfire, hissing and crackling are sufficient, but if a house is burning, the roaring is the most important ingredient.

CHAPTER VI

Animal Sounds

(1) *Vocal.* This would appear to be an almost in-
exhaustible subject in itself, but luckily it is not,
partly because the kinds of animals that make noises
in plays are fairly limited, and partly because it is
not possible to describe exactly how vocal mimicry
should be done. The only advice that can be given
to intending mimics is that they should pay a visit
to the beast or bird in question.

Domestic animals figure most in off-stage effects,
and most of them are easy to imitate. The horse
alone presents any serious difficulty, because it has
such a large compass. For a man, the best way to
produce a neigh is to start on his highest falsetto
note and descend rapidly to his lowest, and to finish
the last deep part of the neigh in his natural register,
but on the intake of breath, since he will have
exhausted his supply on the falsetto part. A woman
or a boy could probably neigh more easily. I myself
was more successful before my voice broke, but I
had developed at that time an indescribable guttural
voice, which gave me the depth for the finish.

Apart from domestic animals, certain beasts of
prey are favoured by dramatists. If a census were
taken, the lion and the wolf would probably be
found the most popular. At any rate, the total range

of wild animals called for is not great. In these days of sound travel films, those who have not had the opportunity of visiting foreign parts can study the beasts almost at first hand. This is naturally a great help, since zoological gardens are not always within reach, and, if a special journey is made, it is safe to bet that the particular creature will be asleep.

But when the sound of an animal is not known and there is no means of finding out about it, the only thing to do is to draw upon one's imagination and utter with confidence, trusting that no one in the audience will know better.

There is one device for making a lion's roar, which is worth describing, for when a lion is supposed to be close at hand, its roar is too loud for any human voice to imitate, and this device will overcome the difficulty. Both heads of a small barrel are removed, one of them being replaced with a head of three-ply wood. A longish stout string is passed through a hole bored in the centre of this head and knotted on the outside, so that it will not pull through. The string is thoroughly impregnated with resin, and is held taut with the left hand, while a piece of resinous leather or cloth is pinched round it inside the barrel with the right hand and drawn along it. The resin causes the leather to travel with a stuttering motion along the string, which in turn imparts the vibrations to the head, and these are amplified by the barrel. Thus it "will roar that it will do any man's heart good to hear it"; and, moreover, adapting Bottom's words still further, you can "aggravate its voice, so that it will roar you as gently as any sucking dove".

Careful note should be taken of this device, since it has other uses, which will be explained later.

Often the voice can be amplified sufficiently with some form of megaphone, and the mimicry is greatly assisted by one of the right material. The sound of the voice is qualified by what may be called the key-note of the resonator used. There is a metallic quality in the lowing of a cow; the effectsman should therefore moo through a tin megaphone or into a bucket. His voice will be amplified and at the same time become more metallic. Similarly, the cooing of a pigeon should be done into a wooden or cardboard resonator or into the cupped hands. When amplification is needed and ringing resonance, but without metallic quality, an oil-lamp chimney is the thing to use. It is specially good for roaring and snarling noises.

Many times the reverse of amplification is desired. The voice must be muffled to suggest that the creature is at a distance, or the sound may be one which it is difficult for the human voice to produce as quietly as it really is; or, again, special circumstances, such as a very small stage, thinness of scenery, and the proximity of the audience, may demand that the sound be toned down. In these cases also the material of the "mute", whatever it is, ought to be considered and chosen to suit the sound that is to be made. Naturally these remarks are also applicable to sounds other than animal sounds.

The bird-whistle should not be passed over without mention. I am not a virtuoso on this instrument, nor do I claim to have exploited its potentialities fully, but it does not seem possible to get more than bubble and/or squeak out of it. By its very nature, being a fixed whistle, it cannot yield more than one note, and most birds have several. A good bird-mimic is infinitely preferable.

The hooting of an owl, and incidentally a train whistle, is produced by clasping the hands tightly and blowing through the narrow space between the thumbs. The upper lip rests upon the top of the bent thumb-knuckles.

The position with regard to records of bird and animal sounds is somewhat strange. Some are so excellent and some so unbelievably bad. Columbia YB19 records the song of the blackbird, nightingale, and canary, each single, and each good, but with one exception there are no records of birds' song generally, which would be so valuable for giving atmosphere, such as birds waking in a garden, and sea-gulls, and rooks. The exception is H.M.V. B3345, Daybreak at a Surrey Farm (birds and animals), the use of which is limited, and on the other side, In a Village Churchyard (birds, bells, organ and choir), so limited as to be practically useless.

Reverting to animals, Columbia make a good record, YB20, having lion, pigs, donkey (bad), and crying baby on one side, and on the other bear, tiger, and elephants, a truly Biblical collection. YB21 is good also of various kinds of dogs barking, dog-fight, and dog run over. YB19, to which I have referred, has duck (single and patently bogus), cock and hens (very good), and cats (bad). A pack of hounds is also available, YB15. The other domestic animals occur only in the Surrey Farm record and are very difficult to pick out, if needed singly, unless one of the special radiograms made for theatrical work is being used, which have a pointer, a graduated scale fixed to the tone-arm, and also a lever attachment, whereby the needle can be lowered accurately into the correct groove. Nor is the wolf recorded either singly or in the pack. Consequently there is still a great deal of fun left in the effectsman's life; the business has not yet been ruined by mechanization.

(2) *Bodily*. (*a*) Of bodily sounds, both human and animal, perhaps the most used is that of horse-hooves. It is generally known that the implements for this effect are the two halves of a coco-nut-shell, though betel picnic cups or small wooden bowls will do equally well. These, and a surface on which to perform, carefully chosen to suit the occasion, complete the equipment. All that is necessary then is an accurate knowledge of how a horse puts its feet to the ground at its various gaits. This is, of course, the crux of the matter, for faulty timing will ruin the effect. Particular attention should be paid to the changes from one gait to another.

Most saddle- and carriage-horses can be imitated with one pair of coco-nut-shells only. The cart-horse effect, to which reference was made in Chapter IV, caused me some trouble, however. After wandering round the theatre for a long time thumping everything, I discovered eventually that the only way to achieve the correct rhythm and weight of the beast was to proceed on hands and feet in the most un-dignified manner. The stage-cloth happened to be laid over a thick felt, which made a very good "dead" surface, and the "horse" was shod with coconuts before and brogues behind. He wore a necklace of light chain to give harness-jingle. When the scene was set, there was very little space on the stage-cloth off-stage, which cramped his manœuvres considerably, so that the audible success of the effect was as nothing to its beauty as a spectacle.

Another method has just suggested itself at the moment of writing, and proves by experiment to be very successful, namely, to sit on the edge of a chair wearing ordinary walking-shoes, with one's feet on a mat. Then the hoof-beats can be made with betel mugs actually on the shoes, which provide in a small compass a very good range of surfaces, for the toe-caps are semi-hard, the instep and sides soft, and the heel hard. Also, if weight is needed, the feet can be brought into play as well without the fatigue of the all-fours method.

(b) Another bodily sound that can be most effective is that of flapping wings. Some birds, pigeons for instance, make flapping sounds, as they launch themselves into flight. This sound can easily be made by holding a folded newspaper in one hand and slapping the corner of it rapidly with the fingers of the other.

The noise of the wings of a frightened hen can be made by flapping a large cotton handkerchief violently. If this is done in a ply-wood chest or against wire-netting and supplemented with frenzied clucking, a splendid backyard illusion is created.

The sound of a flight of birds passing is generally like a deep-toned gust of wind, though there are exceptions, and the wind-machine will supply it.

(c) Sometimes bodily sounds are helpful, when made in conjunction with vocal mimicry, or instead of it, if the effectsman cannot copy a given animal successfully. For instance, the sound of an animal being patted is very suggestive.

To represent the patting of a sleek animal, the thigh with the clothing held taut over it should be slapped, but slapping the chest suggests a shaggy beast better, since it gives a deeper, woollier note.

In "Midsummer Eve" I had to establish the presence of an ailing cow in a stable adjoining the barn, and it was evident that to start with nothing but a moaning sound, when the curtain rose, would not suggest anything clear. Moreover, it was essential that no humorous element should be allowed to creep in. So I decided to establish "cow" first, leaving the "sickness" till a later cue. I had a hollow box-seat, a length of chain trailing over it, and a tin megaphone. I sat on the box, and first drew the chain along a little, to suggest that the cow was turning its head. I chose chain, although its use was improbable, to ensure that the sound carried. Almost at the same time I kicked the seat with my heel two or three times, as though the cow were kicking the side of the stall, and finally moo-ed into the megaphone. The mooing suggested "cow" and the other sounds its restlessness. That done I could make the cow progressively sicker at each utterance, until it died, but even so it was difficult to make it sound genuine and not laughable. The sounds had to be made with the greatest sincerity. One had to play the part of that animal in pain for all one was worth, never daring for a moment to think of the ridiculous aspect of the matter. It was an interesting experience, for it proved conclusively that in the theatre the performer's mental attitude is of paramount importance.

CHAPTER VII

Explosive Sounds

(1) *Big Explosions*. The usual way of making a big explosion is to fire a maroon electrically. The maroon must be placed in a tank covered with wire-netting of small mesh, to prevent burning debris being blown about the stage. The maroons are obtainable in various sizes from the manufacturers of fireworks. The price of course varies with the size, but one shilling will purchase a bang loud enough for most occasions. The stage-lighting firms also supply them and will let out on hire the necessary tank and electrical equipment.

Another method is simply to discharge a twelve-bore shotgun loaded with blank cartridges into a tank. This is a more satisfactory method on the whole. The sound is very loud even in a large theatre, and there is less danger, since the discharge can be directed. Moreover, electricity is temperamental stuff, and accidents are likely to happen, unless the wiring is expertly prepared, but a shotgun in the hands of any intelligent person behaves instantly, safely, and with certainty. Misfires are rare, provided the cartridges are fresh, and in any case there is always the second barrel to fall back on, should the first fail. In the recent production of "Red Dawn" at the Globe Theatre, maroons were used, **but a man stood ready with a shotgun in case they failed.**

Whichever method is employed, it is well to avoid making the explosion actually on the stage. It should be made in an adjoining room or passage, so that the door leading to the stage can be closed immediately afterwards, for the fumes are very unpleasant and trying to the voice.

Sometimes the shotgun explosion is too abrupt, as, for instance, when the effect represents the blowing up of a ship or factory. There should be reverberations, and these can be supplied by a diminuendo roll on a bass drum. Also it gives the stage-manager a comfortable feeling to know that the drum is at hand in the unlikely event of both barrels of the gun missing fire. If a drum is not available, a tea-chest is a possible substitute.

In very distant explosions the reverberations are not heard; the sound is a dull thud. The drumstick or soft underside of the closed fist should be brought down on the drumhead, and held there to kill the vibrations. "Bump" instead of "Boom".

(2) *Artillery.* The same methods are used as for big explosions. This becomes very expensive, however, if a bombardment is to be staged. A Service revolver might be successful, as it makes a loud noise indoors. It has this advantage, too, over a gun, that it needs to be reloaded less often. But in country places such a thing might be hard to get, and even in towns the necessary blank ammunition would be practically impossible to obtain. The only places at which one can be sure of getting it are the London gunsmiths, who cater for theatrical requirements. Then, too, a firearms certificate (5s.) is necessary,

properly made out either for revolver or shotgun, before one can have either in one's possession or buy ammunition.

The only answer to this bombardment question for ordinary societies seems to be the use of bombardment records. These are not good, because the sound is greater than a microphone can take in, and a great deal of distortion results. But such a record would provide a weighty background of sound, which could be supplemented with musketry and machine-gun effects, and with careful work on a bass drum. A point in favour of records is this, that, being a reproduction of the real thing, they include the echoes and reverberations natural out of doors and so hard to fake indoors. I believe that they could be faked with a thunder-sheet of very thin metal or with a sheet of ply-wood, but the record is the simplest means for general purposes. (H.M.V. E576.)

Special cases no doubt occur, in which the shell-bursts have to be fitted in with the dialogue. For these a record would not serve, and it would be most interesting to work out an effect on a large scale. It would require performers of more than average ability to ensure that the battle did not degenerate into an ordinary thunderstorm. It would be wise for the producer to get expert assistance, if he has not himself experienced shell-fire, for there are many who have, and knowledgeable persons in the audience will be offended if the sounds are not true. The trench-mortar shell must arrive with its own peculiar rhythmic sob, and the various field-gun shells must have each its proper whine. For this latter effect the siren whistle is not to be commended.

Most people can recognize it for what it is, and it has too clear a note in any case. The real shell sound is a much more breathy, tearing noise, and is better made by whistling through the fingers after the manner of rude fellows in the street or theatre gallery.

(3) *Small Arms.* The safety pistol is a great asset for theatre work. It is obtainable everywhere with its ammunition. It is cheap and requires no firearms certificate. It is suitable on most occasions, but there are some points worth noting about it. First, if one is being bought to go into the society's stock of properties, it is best to select a fairly expensive one, as it will be more carefully made and finished and therefore less likely to jam. A large one should also be chosen, that can be used as a property on the stage. The small ones look ridiculous when used to threaten. Thirdly, it must be taken to pieces and oiled carefully at regular intervals. This is true of all firearms, but particularly of the safety pistol, because its very cheapness of construction and material render it more liable to damage through neglect.

When a pistol is to be fired on or off the stage, it is a golden rule that it should be fully loaded, even if only one shot is to be fired. It is so depressing, if the hammer descends on an empty chamber, or the single load misses fire.

There is a grim tale that emphasizes this point. In a certain drama the villain has to threaten with a revolver and say, "Do so and so, or I'll shoot you like that!" He fires and smashes a picture. Curtain. The effect was worked by the stage-manager mounted on a step-ladder outside the scene behind the picture, which he smashed by striking with a hammer an iron rod passed through the scenery. The shot and the smash naturally had to be simultaneous. On the occasion in question the revolver, though fully loaded, missed fire no less than five times. Happily, the last round went off, but imagine the sensations of the stage-manager.

Another story comes to mind of a pistol mishap in a performance of "The Queen was in the Parlour" by Noel Coward. For some reason, now forgotten, when the cue came in the last scene, there was no shot off-stage. "General Krish", after momentary hesitation, made his exit, and presently re-entered with a very strained expression to announce, "Your Majesty, a man has cut his throat in the bedroom!"

Often a weapon is supposed to be fired on-stage, but the actual explosion takes place off-stage. The safety pistol is frequently useless for this purpose. Its cartridge is after all no more than a large cap, and the disproportion between its sound and, say, a rifle or ·45 revolver is so marked as to be ludicrous. Consequently a larger weapon must be procured. The blank ammunition of a rifle or ·45 makes too great a noise indoors, when used to represent itself. The charges can be reduced, but it is simpler and less expensive to use a ·32 revolver.

Here again we meet the necessity of having a firearms certificate, and for an active society that is frequently doing plays in which firearms are needed, I would advise that the secretary take out a certificate, made out in his own name, allowing him, not to own, but **to have in his possession** a number of undescribed firearms and to buy blanks up to a reasonable amount, say, one hundred rounds. This will enable him to hire or borrow anything that may be required, and he will not be tied down to any particular kind of weapon. The certificate only costs five shillings and is valid for three years.

Distant rifle or revolver shots are imitated by whacking stretched material with canes. Drain-cane is best, since it does not split. For the stretched material an old flat is good or an upholstered settee or a hard cushion. Experiment will show which is best for a particular purpose.

A very good effect of even more distant firing can be made by tapping a sheet of tin with a short stick. By alternating these two methods one man can represent two sides of an engagement with great facility.

For a volley in a prison-yard, as in "The House with the Twisty Windows", I would suggest mixing the two methods. Four canes descending hard on stretched canvas and one on a thunder-sheet should do it. The latter should give the flat parade-ground echo. Indeed, the mixture of surfaces is worth investigation for any effect, in which firing is supposed to take place among buildings. In a revolutionary scene, for example, there might be a party (a) in the house or room in which the scene is set, another (b) round the corner, another (c) up a side-street, and another (d) across the square opposite. The shots from each party would sound different, so safety pistols could be used for (a), canes on canvas for (b), canes on ply-wood for (c), and sticks on tin for (d).

The same principles apply to machine-gun effects. Those at hand go rot-tot-tot-tot-tot, while those of the enemy go rat-tat-tat-tat. It is possible to hire elaborate mechanisms which work in the same way as the alarm rattle. A wheel with long teeth is turned by a handle and the teeth engage in turn with a strip of springy wood causing it to smack rhythmically. Two such arrangements are enclosed in one box, tuned differently one for the rots and one for the rats. But it is perfectly simple to do the tapping directly by hand with a pencil or ruler on suitable boxes. It is easiest to tap with the arm fully extended, for as soon as the arm is bent it becomes more tiring and the regular rhythm suffers.

As I was writing this I suddenly heard a machine-gun practising on a range some miles distant, and rushed out of doors to listen. The country round is wooded, and the sound was not sharp, but blanketed. In fact, canes on a stretched blanket would reproduce it exactly.

(4) *Miscellaneous Small Explosions.* There are a few other explosive sounds that occur from time to time. Perhaps the most frequent is the popping of a cork. The most reliable way of doing this is with a child's pop-gun. If it misses fire, a second attempt can be made almost instantly, whereas if an actual cork drawn from a bottle misses fire, it cannot be replaced quickly enough.

For the back-firing of a petrol engine there is the pistol for near effects, bursting a paper bag for a more distant one, and canes on canvas or a cushion for the most distant. The last two also serve for a popping gas-fire.

With regard to fireworks, since use of the actual things is seldom permitted, the hissing must be done with a cylinder of air or by relays of people, while the explosions are produced in the various ways described according to the distance and particular fireworks. A pat with the open hand on a soft cushion is an excellent imitation of the "phut" of a rocket bursting.

CHAPTER VIII

Miscellaneous Sounds

(1) *Horns and Sirens*. The records of these effects are very good. H.M.V. E582 has on one side (*a*) Works siren; (*b*) Klaxon horn; (*c*) Electric horn; (*d*) Taxi horn; (*e*) Taxi horn; (*f*) Steamboat siren intermittent; (*g*) Steamboat siren continuous. On the other side are various bugle calls. Columbia YB 5 has on one side airplane effects, and on the other Sirens—(1) Factory; (2) Liner; (3) Tug; (4) Distant Steamboat. This is a fine collection from which to choose, and the sounds record truly.

Most needs of this kind will be met by records, but it is wise to consider other ways of producing these sounds for times when some special effect is wanted.

(*a*) *Horns*. The first point to note about the motor-horn is that it must belong to the car. That is to say, first, that the sounds of the car and the horn must appear to come from the same point in space, even if one has to be made at the side of the stage and the other in a dressing-room; and, secondly, that the horn must be of a type suitable to the kind of car. It should be self-evident that the approach of a Rolls-Royce should not be heralded by the bovine lament of an asthmatic bulb-horn, but it is quite remarkable how often this gross error is perpetrated.

Even if the precise make of car is not disclosed, the status of the owner is usually known, and his car must be selected to suggest this status with just the same care as are his clothes and other properties. Nowadays the horn is a standard fitting on a car, so that the very sound of it should give the audience a clue to the personality of the new arrival. It is possible for a discriminating ear to tell from the horn what sort of vehicle is approaching, and sometimes even its make, for as a general rule each make of car has its own make of horn. In matters theatrical it is not necessary to carry things to such extremities, but a little ordinary commonsense would not be out of place.

One particularly vile device of the care-free effectsman is to stand immediately outside the flimsy scenery and produce a blatant "Honk! honk!" with the full force of his horn, while making no attempt whatever to suggest the engine-sounds that should accompany it. This convention sufficed in the good old days, but an audience fed on the realism of the cinema invariably laughs. If no car effect is available, the horn must be so remote that the sounds of the car from which it comes would reasonably be inaudible.

A loose electric horn and battery can usually be hired from a garage, but, of course, the simplest plan is to use an actual car outside, when local conditions permit.

Failing all else, vocal mimicry is by no means impossible.

(b) *Sirens*. The question of sirens is twofold. How to raise enough wind? And, through what to direct it? The answer to the latter is an organ-pipe. This can be borrowed from the local organ (provided that the organist is properly aware of the importance of The Drama in Village Life, and so forth). There is no technical difficulty, because the pipes merely rest in slots and can be lifted out. The only disaster likely to happen is, that in the excitement of the final Saturday night performance their replacement should be overlooked, causing a rift in the lute at matins. They can also be hired from stage-lighting firms.

Pipes of high pitch can be blown by human lungs, but for ones whose note is low enough for an ordinary ship's siren a store of wind must be found. A cylinder of air is, of course, perfect. Failing that, the inflated mattress might serve, but I doubt if it would work unless skilfully adapted, because the outlet is too small to allow sufficient wind to escape at once. And if it were enlarged, the problem would then arise as to how to apply enough uniform pressure.

The better plan would be to use bellows, the normal method of blowing organ-pipes. It should not be difficult to construct two pairs of bellows, fixed on a stand and worked by hand or pedals, both of which supply a central channel, into which the pipe or pipes are fitted. Or one of those small portable harmoniums, that are occasionally to be seen being played in the street, could be adapted. There is then an unlimited supply of compressed air at command for this or any other purpose, and everything is under instant control.

These suggestions are only theoretical, as I have never had cause to experiment with bellows. But I have discussed the matter with a maker of organs.

He showed me that the flexible joints are made of sheepskin in real bellows, but agreed that strips of rubber ground-sheet would serve for theatrical purposes, when the bellows would not have very hard wear, and when the question of expense is ever-present.

The only time I was faced with this problem, it had been solved already, and in quite a different way. I was stage-managing a production of "R. U. R." in a repertory season. A very loud factory siren is required in this play, but I found that amateurs had already produced it at the same theatre, so that I had simply to follow their method. The management of the theatre possessed a very large vacuum-cleaner on wheels, which could be converted into a blower at will. This was placed in the basement under the stage and a long flexible pipe led up from its blowing orifice through one of the electric dips to the stage. The top end of the pipe was fitted into one side of a small wooden box, from the other side of which sprouted five small organ pipes of different notes. One had simply to switch on the vacuum-cleaner and the noise grew rapidly from a breathing moan to an excruciating clamour, which completely killed the sound of the vacuum-cleaner.

There seems to be no reason why this principle should not be adapted to other circumstances. Certain types of household vacuum-cleaner will convert to blowers. There will be only one difficulty to be overcome. If the sound of the cleaner is out-of-place in the setting and the noise to be made is not loud enough to mask it, the cleaner must be placed out of earshot with a long pipe leading to the stage.

There is one other kind of siren that should be mentioned, the kind used on American police cars. There are good records of this effect, H.M.V. E578 and Columbia YB1.

In this department again vocal mimicry can be entirely satisfactory, even for the last-mentioned effect.

(2) *Chimes*. The records of chimes are deceptive. They give the quarter, half-hour, and three-quarter chimes, but the only hour recorded is twelve, the idea being, I suppose, that for other hours the needle should be lifted after the required number of strokes. But the vibrations of one stroke always overlap the next stroke, and to remove the needle or execute a rapid fade-out will bring the vibrations to an unnaturally abrupt end, which will certainly destroy the illusion. The hours can be struck on a separate bell, the needle being lifted under cover of the first stroke, but this bell must be one of the correct note, a difficult matter considering that most of the records are of Big Ben. Moreover, what is to be done, if the effect wanted is of a simple village clock? Big Ben would be miscast in the part.

The proper way of dealing with this problem is to hire a set of tubular bells, such as are used in orchestras. A set comprises an octave of bells hung vertically in a wooden trestle-stand. The sets are made in various keys, though that is seldom of importance in off-stage work. The bells are struck at the very top with a special mallet. On such a set naturally a great variety of effects can be produced.

Unfortunately a set of this kind is very expensive and, except in places where orchestras abound, is difficult to obtain. But it satisfies this particular need so perfectly, that a truly exhaustive search should be made in the hope of hiring or borrowing one. The musical instrument firms in London will, of course, supply one, if the society can afford it.

But what can a society do, which cannot get one for love, and has no money? The only way out of the difficulty that I can suggest is to obtain permission from the local ironmonger or electrical contractor to go into his warehouse and hammer the various lengths and sizes of piping that he has in stock. Brass tubing gives the most melodious sound.

In the proper sets of bells the different notes are achieved by difference in the length of the tubes; the longer the tube, the deeper the note. In order that a bell shall ring melodiously and have the proper pitch, the material of which it is made must be of very good quality, there must be no hint of a flaw in the casting, and its length must be absolutely accurate. It is these three factors that make the cost so high. Consequently by the rough and ready method of banging about in a warehouse one cannot expect to pick up a perfect carillon for next to nothing, but one can without much difficulty select a simple clock-chime that will pass muster.

The proper bells are hung in the following manner. A hole is drilled through the tube about one inch from the end. A short length of stout blind-cord is passed through it and its ends are tied together to form a loop. Two cup-hooks are screwed into the underside of the stand's crossbar some three inches apart, and the loop is hung over them both. This method prevents the cord from hugging the top of the bell and damping its vibrations, and should therefore be adopted in hanging any tubes.

Sometimes the effect of a single tolling bell is needed, and it may be inconvenient for some reason to hang it. It has to be held up by hand therefore, and there is considerable strain in holding a long bell clear of the floor for any length of time. But if a comfortable handle is made with a short piece of wood having a hole at each end through which the cord is passed (which incidentally serves the same purpose as the cup-hooks in keeping the cord clear of the bell), and the ringer stands on a chair, he can rest his left elbow on his hip, and in this position hold quite a heavy bell comfortably for as long as is necessary without danger of sagging, his mind being free to concentrate upon striking it with unvarying force and in strict tempo.

(3) *Felling Trees*. This effect is very seldom called for, but I have met it in the last scene of "The Cherry Orchard". I provided a fairly heavy log and a felling-axe and proceeded to chop in a passage just off the stage. The effect was a dismal failure. The sound was much too heavy for indoors. After experiment the sound was finally made by chopping the edge of a piece of three-plywood with a claw-hammer. The plywood was approximately two feet square, and rested on the stage. The hammer was allowed to fall upon it, so that the upper edge went into the fork of the claw. By twisting the hammer occasionally one could tear away pieces of the wood, giving just the right rending sound.

When a tree falls, a particularly loud crack must be made in this way, followed by a swish with a wind-machine, and a crunch. For a distant effect I suggest that the crunch could be made by stepping heavily with one foot into a box or basket partly filled with crackly brown paper. For closer effects the sound could be magnified by dropping a heavy weight into the box, across the top of which plasterer's lathes had been laid. The bottom of the box should be padded, so that the ultimate thud is soft and earthy.

If there is no wind-machine at hand to make the swish, a stiff broom or besom could be swept along an old flat or the wall.

(4) *Breaking Harp-string Effect in "The Cherry Orchard"*. As I have mentioned this effect earlier, I must tell how it was done at the Old Vic, namely, with a musical saw. Any ordinary saw, except of course a tenon saw, will make a similar sound, but a proper musical saw gives the best results, being longer, heavier, and of special temper. For these reasons it is an expensive article, the cheapest costing fifteen shillings.

To play the saw the performer sits gripping the handle between his knees. He grasps the other end and bends it over to the left. It is important that the bend should be correct. Having bent the blade over and down, he must bend the end upwards again, as though he were trying to snap it off, thus forcing the saw into an S curvature. He can then play it, either by striking the flat of the blade on its convex curve with a small padded stick (the method used for the harp-string effect) or by bowing with a 'cello bow on the smooth edge.

The sounds produced are marvellously eerie and good use can be made of them in "spook" plays. I have played this instrument in the cauldron scene of "Macbeth", and have had a part written for it in incidental music for "The Tempest".

(5) *Marching*. A regiment cannot be suggested by four people marking time on boards. But, if they will steady themselves with one hand and swing one foot, so that it slips across the floor rhythmically to and fro, the effect is quite good. However, a small cardboard box, e.g. a wig box, containing a quantity of coke, rice, or peas, when shaken from side to side, produces the effect in the best and simplest way, only one person being needed to work it. It is not easy to make it fade in and out, so the producer must arrange his production in such a way that the effectsman can approach and retire out of earshot in the right directions.

(6) *Approaching and Departing Footsteps*. Much more thought and trouble should be taken in this matter of footsteps. The illusion is ruined when the the feet of a character making an exit into the garden are heard thumping on boards. As previously stated, silence is better than the wrong sound. I would suggest therefore that, if the lawn may be supposed to begin immediately outside the window of the set, an old rug or a sack be laid down for the characters to step on. If there is a gallery in the theatre, and the space to be so carpeted is visible, it is a simple matter to cover the carpet with painted canvas. Good use could also be made of the gravel box and perhaps of tiles, slates, or sheet asbestos to suggest what lies outside the set.

The attention of the audience is focused mainly upon that which lies before them, but is shifted to what lies outside their line of vision every time an entrance or exit is made. As a rule they are only too ready to use their imaginations, but they cannot do so if they are continually being made conscious of actualities, through lack of imagination on the part of those responsible for the production.

Clearly no hard and fast rule can be laid down about this question of footsteps. One may easily be presented with an insoluble problem, as for instance a centre exit supposed to lead to a crazy-paved terrace in a play full of quick changes. One cannot set and strike crazy-paving in a moment of time. But the question is worth far more serious attention. I believe that there are considerable unexplored possibilities in off-stage footsteps not only in realistic drama but from the point of view of giving atmosphere in all kinds of productions, provided that the matter is handled with reason and artistic restraint.

A difficulty sometimes presents itself, when a play demands that footsteps shall be heard over-head. In a proper theatre sounds can be made on the fly-floor and all is well, but in most small halls there is no means of getting up over the stage even at one side. It is at the same time much easier to locate the source of a sound in a small theatre, for in a big place the echoes confuse the ear; it is the more necessary therefore that an effect shall come from the right direction.

The usual practice is to make the sounds on the stage up centre behind the set. This is the best thing to do in most cases. The sounds, however, should not be like those of ordinary footsteps, but muffled, since they are supposed to be heard through a floor and ceiling. These muffled sounds, assisted by the players acting as though they came from upstairs, should satisfy.

It might be possible to fix a box above the set and make sounds upon it with a padded weight, worked from the side of the stage by a cord running over pulleys, but only footsteps or light sounds could be made. The contrivance would be useless for effects such as that in "The Importance of being Earnest", Act III, when Jack Worthing hurls trunks about in his search for the handbag.

If then the circumstances dictate that the sounds must be made on the stage itself, the most important points are that they should come from the right horizontal direction and be suitably muffled.

(7) *Creaks and Squeaks.* Creaks are simple to produce. The lion-roaring apparatus, described in Chapter VI, embodies the principle of creak-making. Questions of size of apparatus are governed by the needs of the moments and the materials at hand. I used two such creak-tubs in the shipwreck scene of "The Tempest", to suggest groaning timbers and cordage. One was a cheese-barrel, unaltered except for the resined string, the other was a small oyster-barrel approximately fourteen inches long and seven inches in diameter, which had already done duty as a tabor. For the latter purpose it ends had been removed and drumheads of parchment substituted. I took off one head and passed the string through a hole in the other, tying its end round a chip of wood to prevent it pulling through.

The first and larger of these two tubs gave a deep note excellent for straining timbers. It would be suitable for the sound of a boat rubbing against a landing-stage, or for the shuddering moan of a heavy prison door. The latter by reason of its parchment head gave the light creak of rigging, but, when worked with violence, was capable of producing an excruciating shriek. A tub of this kind would be a useful component in a train-wreck and similar effects.

Another method, very simple yet most effective, is to twist an ordinary toy balloon between the hands. Yet, if an effectsman were depending on this method, and an accident happened to his balloon during the performance, he would do well to remember that creaks can also be made by pushing his finger tip across any smooth wooden surface.

Squeaks are more difficult to produce, because their pitch is higher and more musical, and unless the method is well conceived, they easily degenerate into creaks. For the important gate-squeak in "The Fanatics", after fruitless hours spent in a scrap-iron yard trying to find two pieces that would squeak together infallibly, I finally made an attempt at it with a violin by bowing on the wrong side of the bridge. But in spite of the vile noise that resulted, the violin was still recognizable. By more recent experiment I find that a good reliable squeak can be made with a piece of resined string and a drawer.

The small top drawer of an ordinary chest of drawers is a convenient size for the purpose. One end of the string is looped over the drawer-knob, and the other is tied round a short wooden handle. The performer holds the handle in one hand and strains the string across the aperture of the drawer, but not too tightly. He pinches the string between the finger and thumb of the other hand **lightly** and draws his hand along it. A minute's practice will suffice to discover the proper tension and pressure.

Squeaks can also be made by stirring the tip of a penknife on a china plate. The knife must be held at right angles to the plate. By reason of the rotary motion, this method is good for imitating car-brakes, but it is only suitable in a small hall.

It is possible as well to mimic squeaks by whistling. The musical squeak of a door-hinge can be imitated by anyone who can whistle very high notes in the ordinary way, while the peculiar whirring squeak of a car skidding with locked brakes can be done by whistling through the fingers, especially if the whistling is breathy, and if the tongue is fluttered at the same time

(8) *Halyards*. The sound of halyards slapping against a mast is done, as would be expected, by fastening one end of a length of cord to a batten and working the slapping from the other end. I mention it only because, for a simple sound, it gives such extraordinarily good atmosphere.

(9) *Trumpets*. Although really music cues, it may be valuable to discuss trumpet-calls here, since they present considerable difficulty. By "trumpet-calls" I mean not bugle-calls, réveillé, the Last Post, and so forth, but those single blasts and fanfares that occur in Shakespeare and costume plays generally.

Expert trumpeters are scarce, and even an ordinarily competent player, who can keep his end up in orchestral work, will often be found wanting when working to cue, especially if asked to start on a high note, before he is "warmed up". It is obviously disastrous to a dramatic or poignant moment, if the clarion notes have haloes round them.

Records are unsatisfactory. The trumpet does not record well, and the small range of fanfares obtainable, besides being too long for many occasions,

give a very strong suggestion of modern pageantry.
As one listens to them, one can almost see the
Temple and the Mansion House. They are therefore unsuitable on such occasions as Othello's
arrival in Cyprus, or the last scene of "The Merchant
of Venice", "My husband is at hand. I know his
trumpet"; or "The Tragedy of Nan", Act III,
"The 'orn, the 'orn, the gold rider be comin'."

So what is to be done? In the first place vocal
mimicry is not to be despised. A few notes uttered
with the confidence born of practice, through a
metal resonator and **with reasonable remoteness**,
will give a very satisfactory result.

I have had to imitate the horn of a Swiss diligence
in this way. I did not know what it should be like,
having never heard one, so I had to make inquiries,
and there was rather a choice moment at the end of
the search, when, because I cannot read music, the
clerk in the London office of Swiss Federal Railways
sang to me across the counter.

Secondly, though I have had no opportunity to
prove this theory, I feel sure that a competent
violinist could produce a presentable fanfare on
one of those single-stringed instruments that have
a horn attached, the proper name of which is Stroh-
viol.

CHAPTER IX

Complex Effects

(1) *Crowds.* In the matter of crowds records are a great assistance. They have the virtue of compactness, and, when used on a radiogram, are under instant and precise control, which is seldom the case with the human element. Columbia offer YB2, Crowd Effect or Angry Mob; Fair Ground—Crowd Effect and Roundabouts, etc. YB3, Cheering Crowd; Clashing Swords and Crowd Murmurs. YB17, (1) Crowd at Races; (2) Angry Crowd at Races. (Other side; Machinery Noises—Printing Press.) YB18, (1) Laughter in Theatre; (2) Applause in Theatre. (Other side: Street Traffic Noises.) The H.M.V. selection consists of E573, In a Theatre, (*a*) Orchestra tuning up; (*b*) Noise of audience; (*c*) Applause; In a Restaurant, (*a*) Noises in a restaurant; (*b*) As above with music. E579, Crowd Scenes, (*a*) General noises; (*b*) Angry crowd; (*c*) Frightened crowd; (Other side) (*a*) Cheering crowd; (*b*) Applause and cheers; (*c*) Laughing crowd.

Actual voices are frequently used with a record and the disabilities of the ordinary gramophone can be overcome by rehearsing them to fade in, to bridge the gap, while the needle is put back, to create a crescendo or climax, and to fade out. When individual lines have to come from the crowd, naturally the use of voices is imperative. It is then a question not of voices assisting the record, but rather of the record being an auxiliary or make-weight to the voices.

All this is fairly simple. The struggle begins when a large number of persons are engaged in crowd effects, and records are dispensed with.

The choice of persons to form a crowd is a very difficult business. I am well aware that it is practically impossible to find oneself in the happy position of being able to select the members of a crowd as one selects the cast. Generally the left-overs have to be used, those other members of the society or company, some of whom perhaps have expected to be given parts and are disgruntled, because the expected has not come to pass. In such circumstances the producer's path is thorny, for though he tells them, with perfect truth, that crowd-work, albeit somewhat dull and thankless, is first-rate experience and vital to the success of the play, they will merely think that he is trying to coax them, which is equally true, and continue to sulk.

If at all possible, I would certainly advise that such malcontents should be allowed to withdraw. For crowd-work undoubtedly is dull and thankless for the most part, but it is also difficult, strenuous, and demands the maximum of alertness and sensitiveness from the performers, and persons carrying an insoluble load of umbrage cannot be expected to give this maximum. Likewise I would make tactful arrangements to dispense with the services of natural comedians. Crowd-work is frequently intensely humorous, especially in tragedies, and the sallies of those who cannot resist the lure of the laugh are generally disastrous.

I have said that crowd-work is dull. What usually happens is this. A collection of **individuals**, in various states of mind, are marshalled into a corner off-stage, or perhaps even into a room or passage quite out of touch with the play. They are asked to make crowd noises in a certain mood. Someone flaps at them, and they begin, some to talk nonsense and giggle, others, the bored ones, sitting or leaning, to utter a doleful growling without life or meaning. They do this a great many times until the volume is right. Then the scene is rehearsed on stage and the crowd take up their cues. Perhaps the scene on the stage is stopped by a "dry-up" or a technical point, but no one stops the crowd. So they go on, until sworn at. Then they miss their cue, because they are talking and do not know that the scene has started again, and so on, and so on. It becomes wearisome, so thinking that they know their cues and what to do, they begin to "cut" rehearsals. The scene is rehearsed without a crowd or with one of only half the proper strength, and the actors grow accustomed to speaking in their normal tones. When the first performance arrives, the crowd, under-rehearsed and fired with the exuberance of the moment, make twice as much noise as they should and the actors are taken by surprise and "swamped".

Even if things do not come to such a pass, it stands to reason that the results of this way of handling a crowd will not have anything approaching their full dramatic or emotional value to the play.

"The crowd" is a unit, a member of the cast and has all the values that a character has, a value as part of the plot, a value as part of the choral scheme of the voices, an atmospheric value, and so forth. It must therefore work as a unit, and clearly that will never be, if the persons who represent "The Crowd" remain a collection of individuals chanting automatically, in utter ignorance of their purpose and effect.

The producer has to bring about the fusion of the individuals into the mass, but in order to gain the maximum of effect with the minimum of vexation, the mass must be willing and keenly responsive. Now, since crowd-work offers no personal reward other than the satisfaction of having done the job well—good old "Art for art's sake!"—the producer must by all means arouse the enthusiasm of the individuals for the business in hand, so that they will consent to sink their own personalities for the good of the cause—good old "Teamwork!"

This means that he must treat them as intelligent beings, not as necessary evils, and explain to them carefully at the first readings of the play his aims and intentions in handling "The Crowd". And further, at the first rehearsals of their scenes, he should bid them sit in front, so that they can see what happens on the stage and exactly how the crowd effects fit in. If the scene is intricate, he might with advantage play the part of "The Crowd" himself as a demonstration. Only after this should the crowd-members be despatched into the wings to try.

The next step is to determine by methodical experiment "The Crowd's" exact position or positions for its various cues and the maximum and minimum volumes of sound that it is to make. Then at last rehearsals proper can begin, the ground having been cleared and prepared.

For the performers there are one or two points to be noted. They may be representing anything from a small group of servants or neighbours gossiping to a vast urban throng of exultant or revolting citizens. In the first case each performer may stand for one member of "The Crowd", and he should then write a part for himself properly characterized with suitable dialogue. In the other case each performer will have to represent ten, twenty, fifty, or one hundred souls, which means that he will have to make not necessarily more noise, but a different kind of noise, a confused burble rather than a single conversation. He may have to represent two sides of a dispute in rapid alternation, punctuated perhaps by isolated, individually characterized lines. Consequently he will have to talk, shout or murmur with as much rapidity and as many changes of voice, pitch and tempo as he can muster, keeping his individual lines clear and definite in his mind, so that they come out with clarity and definition from the background of burble.

What is he to say therefore, since it is not possible to carry on a hundred conversations at once? The best plan is to learn off pat a long speech or poem, which can then flow out of him **indistinctly** and coloured by any necessary mood. I always use the words of the Chancellor's nightmare song from "Iolanthe".

The point is that the words should come automatically, so that the performer can concentrate his attention on the mood and volume of his noise. If he "dries up", he can begin the speech again, but he must not be at a loss for words and let his contribution degenerate into that appalling "Wur! wur! wur!", which is utterly unnatural, and fatal to the effect, which is to be one of blurred speech. "Wur! wur! wur!" is heard nowhere in the world—except in stage crowds.

The sound of a large number of people talking ordinarily, as for instance in a restaurant or theatre, is very like the sound of rain. It would be interesting to experiment with a drum and peas, when a multitude is to be suggested and actual performers are few.

Having discussed this matter from the points of view of both producer and performer, we now arrive at the vital question of liaison between the two. I have already stressed the need for absolute control in off-stage effects. At no time is it more necessary than when dealing with a crowd. Someone therefore must be appointed to conduct, and it is best if he can be exempted from helping to make the noise, for he can then use his ears only to hear the cues and to gauge the volume of sound.

The conductor may be the stage-manager or his assistant, but should they be busy elsewhere, someone else must be appointed. In any case the conductor must be a person of sufficient personality and authority to command the attention of the performers, since the main responsibility rests with him.

An imaginative person in this position can make a crowd tremendously effective by conducting it in the full sense of the word. The orchestral conductor performs not only a unifying function by beating time, but also an interpretive function. The conception of how the music should be played, of its purpose and meaning, of its emotional, intellectual, or pictorial intent, proceeds from his single imagination. The same is true of the crowd-conductor, though of course he is working under the producer, who is the supreme conductor of the whole dramatic effect, and must take his interpretation from him. Yet it often happens that the producer, who is blessed with some sensitive person to conduct the crowd, or indeed any composite effect, resigns to him the creative role, retaining for himself only that of critic. And this method is, I believe, the best, for the crowd-conductor can give of his personal imaginative best unhampered by the need to follow another's instructions. His work will be first-hand. Besides, few persons are capable of expressing in words **exactly what they want** when dealing with anything so imponderable as dramatic value. And, if the crowd-conductor is so much in sympathy with the producer, that he can understand exactly what is wanted, then the need for instructions, explanations, words immediately disappears, and he can safely be left to his own devices.

Moreover, when the play is actually being performed, the producer's active work is finished. (In passing, I should like to say that during the performance, particularly the first, the producer's place is in the auditorium making notes, **not** in the wings worrying.) Now no two performances of a play are ever identical. The actors vary. The audiences vary. The emotional tension therefore varies. Consequently our crowd-conductor must be capable of accompanying the actors with his crowd, just as the orchestral conductor accompanies the operatic singers with his orchestra.

From the foregoing it will appear that the post of crowd-conductor is a very important one, and that the greatest care must be exercised in selecting someone to fill it.

(2) *Composite Effects*. As with crowds, so with effects composed of a number of elements and worked by several persons the same problems occur, and the answer to them is the same. They must be conducted, so that complete control may be exercised both from the unifying and interpretive points of view. But whereas a crowd is a unit, a single instrument, a composite effect resembles more nearly an orchestra. A crowd noise is the product of voices, which, though different from each other, are yet basically the same, since they all proceed from similar sources. A crowd can be compared very closely with an organ. But the composite effect is the product of sounds from different sources, of which the crowd may be, and often is, one. And here the conductor's task at once becomes more complicated, for he has to keep the various different elements balanced with each other in relation to the stage set. He may also have to make them register in continuous harmony with each other, or continuous discord, in quick succession or alternation, in abrupt comparison or contrast. And he may have to produce an inspired medley of all these alternatives carefully timed to fit in with dialogue. So, where crowd-conductor equals organist, composite-effects-conductor equals Sir Henry Wood.

When a very complicated effect is to be arranged, I suggest that the conductor should take a leaf out of the orchestral conductor's book, both figuratively and literally, and make a score for himself.

Before the play goes into rehearsal he and the producer can map out the general arrangement of the effect in its relation to the dialogue, deciding which are the most telling moments for silences, climactic sounds or steady crescendos, and set them out on paper in quasi-musical form. During rehearsals, inspiration and the needs of the moment will etch in the details, and gradually a complete composition will be created, all of which must be noted down. The conductor has then a precise account of what is to be done and can conduct from it instead of having to rely on his memory or creative imagination, either of which may fail him in the excitement of performance. Also the effect will take the same course every time and the actors will know with certainty when to speak, so that no point is lost or blurred.

The question then arises, how is a noise written down? What should the score look like? The answer is that the conductor must suit himself and invent his own notation. Any symbols or squiggles will do, provided that they convey **precise** meaning to him. But he had better initiate his understudy into their meaning in case of accidents.

Let us however invent a tiny scene and compile a score for it as an example. Let us suppose that a city is being attacked by revolutionaries and that the actual scene is being played by two defending snipers at an attic window. The text of the play might read as follows:

The sound of rifles and machine-guns lessens considerably.
GEORGE. They ain't answerin' so much.

BILL. No. Is it the end?
GEORGE. Or a lull before the storm?
BILL. Seems as if . . . What's that?

> *The whine of a shell and its explosion are heard.*

GEORGE. Shells.
BILL. Shells?

> *Another shell arrives. A woman is heard screaming in agony.*

GEORGE. God, it's a woman!

> *The screaming goes on.*

BILL (*suddenly*): I'm going to . . .

> *He aims and fires. The screaming stops abruptly.*

> *Another shell arrives.*

GEORGE (*shouting*): The *dirty* . . . !

This is a simple example arranged so that the method of scoring shall be easily understood. The score (Fig. 8) is divided into bars by heavily ruled lines, and each bar is subdivided into beats by faint lines. The top stave is devoted to rifle-fire, the top two lines to the attackers, the bottom two to the defenders. The attackers' rifles are divided again into (top line) stick and sheet of tin (Tang), (2nd line) cane and canvas (Whack), and the defenders' into (4th line) cane and blanket (Phut), and (5th line) alarm pistol (Bang). Similarly, the second stave records machine-guns (top line), attackers' (Rat-tat), (bottom line) defenders', (Rot-tot). The third stave is allotted to dialogue, and the fourth contains the other sounds, the whine and explosion of shells, the screaming, and the fall of glass and masonry.

Thus we get a fairly accurate plan of the whole composite effect at a glance. But it is only fairly accurate, since the timing of the shots is merely suggested, not precisely stated. This could be done, however, by borrowing from musical notation more extensively.

It is, I think, evident from this example that some such method of scoring simplifies the conducting of a big effect, and "can be adapted to almost any occasion, joyful or, as in the present case, distressing".

And could we not take the next logical step? Why not make band parts for the performers?

(3) *Battles*. The subject of modern battles has been covered already in various parts of this book, but nothing has yet been said about antique conflicts. They are very difficult to reproduce convincingly. The clashing of armour and the cries of triumph and defeat have a way of sounding like a drunken domestic staff wrecking the kitchen. For this reason such effects are usually handled in a suggestive rather than a representational manner. Instead of trying to cope with crowd shouts, swords and shields, bow-strings, snapping lances, the hooves of horses and their neighing in terror or pain, words of command, battle cries, groans, marching feet, cartwheels, trumpets and drums, the modern producer generally takes the first and last two ingredients, and with them achieves not an actual battle but an exciting noise. By these means he tries to give the audience the same emotional experience with one-quarter of the labour, at the same time eliminating all risk of ridiculous mishap. Usually he succeeds.

All the same, to arrange a realistic battle effect is one of my ambitions, to prove that it can be done

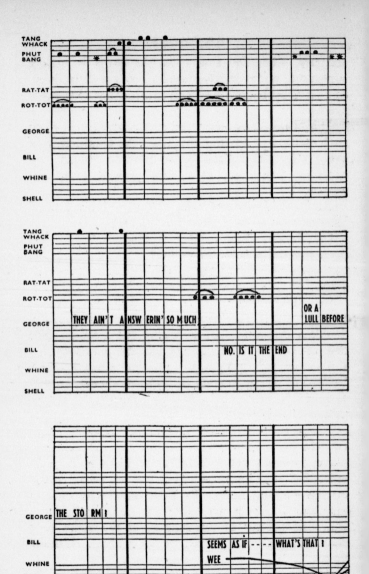

Fig. 8

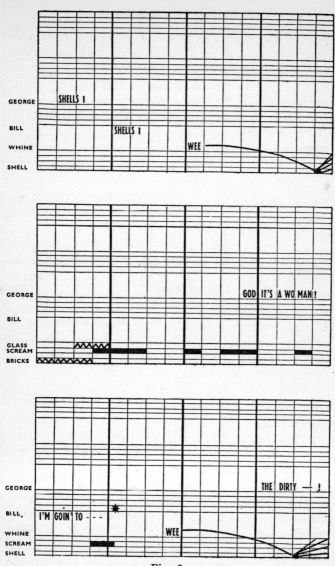

Fig. 8

successfully, and also that the impression on the audience would be far more thrilling than that made by the above labour-saving device. However, I am bound to admit, that if one could achieve an effect that was brilliantly good, the audience would probably begin to think how good it was, and to wonder how it was done, instead of paying attention to the play. An even more probable result would be that all the carefully arranged sounds would coalesce into a smooth hubbub, which, though true to reality, would not sound very different from the usual crowd-and-drum effect. We may take it, then, that the latter plan is the best.

(4) *Formalization*. This simplification of complex effects brings us to another aspect of the matter. In certain kinds of production realism is deliberately avoided in the setting, lighting, acting, and so on. These various branches of dramatic art are treated in some unusual manner suitable to the play that is being produced. Plays about machinery as handled in the Russian Theatre afford an obvious example of this point. In these the actors are, so to speak, mechanized in speech, movement, costume, and make-up. The setting also abounds in geometrical shapes suggesting machinery. Some plays can be produced with the accent on the fantastic or the grotesque. Others, poetic plays, are sometimes handled in the manner of modern ballet and all the movements and gestures become almost those of a formal dance. One hesitates to describe these kinds of treatment as "formalization" or "conventionalization" or "stylization" or any of the other "izations" or "isms", the precise meanings of which are so hard to determine (I have chosen the first for

want of a better), but, whatever they are called, it is clear that the off-stage effects must undergo the same kind of treatment as the rest of the play, otherwise there will be no artistic unity.

It will doubtless be asked, How can a noise off be made in the manner of modern ballet? Visions rise in the mind of artistic youths armed with drumsticks doing arabesques from bass drum to thundersheet. But what I mean is this, that as in the dance natural movement is "tidied up" and arranged to form a pattern, so noises off can be "tidied up" and arranged to form a pattern of sound which approximates to music. Indeed, music is frequently substituted outright for such effects as battles and storms.

In tidying up movement to form a dance the choreographer has to deal with questions of time and space, but in tidying up noise, the only factor is time. Therefore formalized sound effects automatically become rhythmical.

Let us consider some examples. In "Le Viol de Lucrece", by André Obey, the crowd-shouts in the last scene are formalized, and the same treatment is used in Thornton Wilder's translation. Unfortunately I have not seen either version performed, but I am told that in the French production of Michel St. Denis with Le Compagnie des Quinze the crowd was brought on to the stage and employed there more or less continuously in making groupings and poses indicative of sorrow with vocal utterance to match. The vocal utterance was closely comparable to keening, which is simply formal lamentation.

The translation suggests that the crowd should be kept off-stage and used as sound only. The situation in the play is this. Junius Brutus, friend to Lucrece's husband, Collatine, is making a long funeral oration over the body of Lucrece. To this the crowd react not with continuous sound but with single utterances on definite cues. Each member of the crowd cries, "Ha!", tuned to the emotion proper to each moment, so that the total effect of the crowd sound is that of chords punctuating the speech of Brutus, the soloist. It must, I think, be tremendously exciting in performance.

Another example of the same kind of effect, this time on-stage, is afforded by the formal "laughter in court" in the one-act play, "Murder Trial", by Sidney Box. In this instance, whenever the judge makes a joke, all the characters (except the prisoner) laugh in unison, "Ha! Ha! Ha! Ha!", four times on descending notes. The effect, by its very artificiality, is very amusing.

In these three examples it is the fact that the effects are rhythmical, either in themselves or in relation to their context, that gives them their formality.

In searching for an example of a formalized noise off other than a crowd or battle effect I remember that in a certain production of Flecker's "Hassan" that I saw some years ago, the Procession of Protracted Death was presented in this way. A portion of the cyclorama was lit with red, and upon it was cast the shadow of Masruh, the executioner, moving up and down as though in the act of thrashing. The principal sounds that could be heard were the cries of the tortured, the crack of the whip, and a heavy crash of chains on the stage. These sounds were arranged in order, timed with the swing of the shadow, and repeated in a constantly recurring phrase—"Brump! Crack! Scream! Brump! Crack! Scream!" and so on. Pure rhythm.

As it happens the effect was not a success. Though logical, it was done, as I remember, in too heavy-handed a manner. There was no suggestion of the subtleties of torture, which are foreshadowed in the speeches of the Kaliph in the Divan scene. However, that does not alter the fact that it is rhythm that formalizes a sound effect.

Therefore, for any given effect, a rhythm must be found, which does not destroy the recognizable character of the effect. Fortunately this is not difficult, since most sounds are intrinsically rhythmical or can be repeated in a suitable tempo.

CHAPTER X

Drums

SINCE drums figure so largely in off-stage work, it will be valuable perhaps to add a few remarks on their upkeep and use.

A drum should be slackened when not in use, and stored in a cool, dry place.

To tune it up every alternate screw or rope should be tightened in turn. There are always an odd number of these, so that every one will have been handled by the time one has worked round the drum twice. It is better not to tighten any one fully at first, but to work round four times in all. Thus an even strain is maintained on all sides and the hoops are not pulled crooked.

Moderate tightness only is necessary for a bass drum in the ordinary way. Side-drums naturally need to be tighter. This is a simple matter with the screw pattern, but the military pattern demands more attention.

This type has three metal knobs P projecting from its topmost hoop. It is intended that, whenever the drum is placed on the ground, it should be turned upside-down and stood upon these knobs. The drum is thus kept clear of the ground and the ropes are protected from damage at the point where they pass over the upper edge of the hoop.

The correct way in which to tighten the drum is to place it upside-down, to kneel across the bottom hoop and to pull the leather slides upwards against one's own weight. An extra and more comfortable grip can be obtained by passing a handkerchief under the ropes below the slide. Its two ends are brought up outside the slide and wound round the hand, forming thus a stout loop by which the slide is pulled up.

In course of time the rope stretches and it becomes

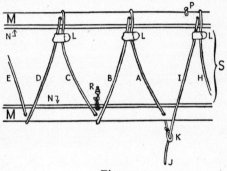

Fig. 9

less and less possible to tighten it sufficiently. The slack that has developed must then be taken up as follows.

The rope is threaded on the drum as illustrated in Fig. 9, which shows the drum flattened out for clarity. The free end J, which is much longer than is shown here, is usually knotted up into a rope chain and allowed to hang in a festoon under the drum. This must all be undone and also the fastening at K. Next, the person doing the job must sit down, remove his shoes, unless they have soft rubber soles, and place the drum on its side between his feet with the rope A on top and the loop K on the right side. He holds the drum down with his feet on the lower inside rims of the hoops and pulls up the ropes in turn, starting with A in the left hand and working round hand over hand till he comes to I, also in the left hand, which leaves his right hand free to take hold of the free end J and make it fast temporarily. The drum rolls round during the operation, so that his feet actually walk round the rims. He will have to repeat the business, starting probably at D and working round to I, and perhaps again, starting at

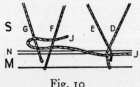

Fig. 10

G, so that he gets a uniform tension all round. He then makes fast permanently.

If there is plenty of free end, it can be used to get extra tension by threading it under D and E near the hoop, and back over E and under D, when a hard tug will pull it out straight, causing D to cross over E (Fig. 10). This should be done all round the drum, but missing out those two ropes between which the snare-hook R lies. Any remaining free end can then be knotted up into a chain again.

The snares are the strings of gut that run from a fixed button on one side of the shell, across the bottom or snarehead to a hook on the other side.

This hook is adjustable for regulating the tension of the snares, so that they snap properly. For many off-stage effects, however, it is necessary to use the drum without them, so they should be slacked off by unscrewing the hook and placing a pad of stuff or paper between them and the snarehead.

The ability to play a drum roll is a valuable asset for an effectsman, so here are instructions for learning to do so.

When a drum is worn by a bandsman on the march, it hangs just in front of his left hip on a slant, the batterhead sloping downwards from left to right. In playing, therefore, the left hand is necessarily higher than the right, and it is from this necessity that the method of holding the sticks originates.

The sticks are held in the forks of the thumbs at the point of balance, i.e. about three and a half inches from the butt-end, so that they will bounce easily. The right hand is held palm downwards, and the stick points to the left, its butt passing under the palm and emerging at the right side near the base of the little finger. The left hand is held palm upwards, and the stick points to the right lying under the thumb, across the bases of the first and middle fingers, and over the back of the other two fingers, which are curled down under it towards the palm (Fig. 11). Both sticks are manipulated by turns of the wrists. When the right hand twists in an anti-clockwise direction, the knob of the stick strikes the drum. When it twists the opposite way, the pad at the base of the little finger presses down the butt and the knob is therefore raised. When the left hand is twisted away from the drum, the back of the third finger lifts the stick off the head. If the pad of the hand were used, the hand would have to twist unnaturally far.

The roll is composed of two beats with each stick alternately in rapid succession, but of course the learner must begin to practise slowly. He should start by striking the drum two separate times slowly with each hand in turn, striving to do it with a turn of the wrist only, while keeping the wrist loose, and continue at this, until the movements become familiar. Then he should gradually increase the

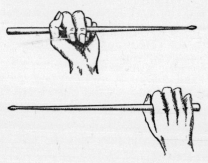

Fig. 11

speed, still keeping the movements easy and the beats regular, until he is tapping as fast as possible. "Tapping", be it noted, not banging. No violence is necessary. Let him practise working up from slow to fast and back again, until he can do it easily.

But there is a limit to the speed at which two separate beats with each hand can be made. It cannot be done fast enough to produce a roll, so the method is changed to that of tapping once and letting the stick bounce once.

The next step is to practise the change, still

keeping the regular rhythm. This is the crux of the whole matter. An accomplished drummer can work up from slow single beats to a tight roll without irregularity or perceptible change of method.

After this has been learnt, all that remains is to practise, until the alternate tap-bounces can be done fast enough to become a roll.

The temptation to try and do this at once without bothering about the early part of the training is very great indeed, but he who gives way to it is very misguided. After all, the movements are strange to a beginner, and the first lessons are designed simply to train his hands methodically to make them. Once that is done, the rest follows with comparative ease. Attempts to make them rapidly at once without training result only in unnecessary fatigue and exasperation.

All this refers only to the side-drum roll. In the tympani and bass-drum rolls the sticks are held one in each hand like hammers and the roll consists of single alternate beats.

Incidentally, when the hands are tired from practising, it is a good plan to shake them hard, as if one was trying to shake them off.

Regarded from the financial point of view the art can be acquired with ridiculous cheapness. A pair of light sticks costs eighteenpence, and a drum is unnecessary, and indeed undesirable. A table-top is better, for it makes far less noise, so that the learner can practise to his heart's content without causing annoyance to any but the other occupants of the house. A drum would rouse the whole parish. Secondly, a table is a harsh critic. The taps upon it are clean-cut, and every unevenness is clearly audible. When practising on a drum, on the other hand, the learner is inclined to think that his progress is vastly better than it is, for in reality the snares are doing half the work.

In off-stage work it is seldom convenient to wear the drum on a proper sling. If the drummer is also playing a part, he may disarrange his clothing or wig in putting on and taking off the sling, or may accidentally make an entrance still wearing it. The simplest plan is to place the drum on a chair, tying it, so that it rests at the proper slope. The sticks should be left together, **head to tail**, lying upon the batterhead, so that when they are taken up in one hand, the butt of one lies in that hand, while the butt of the other is at the other end ready for the other hand. The uninitiated invariably put them down with both butts together. Thus the drummer can, if necessary, walk straight off after his scene and instantly begin playing. Likewise he can leave the drum instantly, without wasting valuable time putting it down noiselessly.

So much for drums. But now I have a few final remarks to make on the subject as a whole. I have already stressed the somewhat obvious point, that, if an effectsman is asked to produce a sound, which is unfamiliar to him, he must take steps to familiarize himself with it, but it might not be amiss to add here, that he should also be cautious with sounds that he believes to be familiar, sounds that he hears every day, for it may well be that he has never really listened to them.

We find here another good reason why noises off should be tackled at the beginning of rehearsals. Producers must be made to grasp the point, that the effectsman requires time to study his part and time for research work.

And here is another reason. The noises are intended to help the actors. It is not impossible to perform a play successfully on a bare stage with no aids to illusion whatever, except chairs. Therefore each thing that is added to a production in the way of scenery, properties, costume, lighting, music, and noises is meant either directly or indirectly to make the actors' work easier. Ideally, the set and everything else should be ready for use at rehearsal by the time the actors are getting rid of their books, so that there would be no need for all those harassing alterations of moves, etc., at the last moment. As things are, however, the compromise of using substitutes, wherever possible, has to be adopted. Substitute noises off can also be used. They are better than nothing. But strenuous efforts should be made to collect the apparatus, so that the correct sounds can be produced at rehearsals for the sake of the actors, whom they are supposed to help. An unexpected noise off at the first performance can be more devastating than anything else. The classic story of the amateur and the pistol-shot bears out this statement. He had only one line to say, "My lord, I hear a pistol-shot." On the first night the pistol was fired for the first time, and he jumped and said, "My God, what's that?"

Finally, if this book has aroused or whetted your interest in the subject, do not allow yourself to be carried away by your enthusiasm. Do not become a crank, and overload your productions with noises. After all, "The play's the thing".